AN INTRODUCTION TO
NEO-COLONIALISM

by
JACK WODDIS

INTERNATIONAL PUBLISHERS

NEW YORK

Dedicated to

VAN TROI
TURCIOS LIMA
BEN BARKA

heroes of three continents who
gave their lives in the struggle to
liberate Vietnam, Guatemala and
Morocco from the chains of
imperialism and neo-colonialism

Contents

EDITOR'S NOTE

The following works, cited in the text, are available in editions issued by International Publishers, New York:

CABRAL, AMILCAR, "National Liberation and the Social Structure," in William J. Pomeroy, ed., *Guerrilla Warfare and Marxism,* 1968.

JAGAN, CHEDDI, *The West on Trial,* 1967.

LENIN, V. I., *Imperialism, The Highest Stage of Capitalism* (new ed.) , 1969.

——*Selected Works* (3 vols.) , 1968.

MAO TSE-TUNG, *Selected Works* (5 vols.) , 1954, 1956.

MARX, KARL, *Capital* (3 vols.) , 1967.

NKRUMAH, KWAME, *Neo-Colonialism: The Last Stage of Imperialism,* 1966.

Introduction

Today the term "neo-colonialism" has entered into common usage in political debate, to such an extent, in fact, that several books specifically concerned with it have already appeared. It is, indeed, well-nigh impossible to hold intelligent discussion with representatives of the "Third World" or to expound on the problems of developing countries without finding oneself in the midst of animated debate about neo-colonialism.

The term neo-colonialism has today become so much a part of the popular terminology of the people of Asia, Africa and Latin America that the most damaging criticism that can be levelled at a political leader in these continents is to charge him with being an agent of neo-colonialism. Yet it was as recently as 1964 that Sir Alec Douglas-Home was asserting that the term "has no place in Britain's political dictionary. We quite simply do not know its meaning."*

In March 1961, the Third All-African People's Conference met in Cairo. Speaker after speaker went to the rostrum to denounce neo-colonialism, and at the end of the conference a special resolution on the subject was adopted. It was clear that for these spokesmen of Africa neo-colonialism certainly had a meaning; for them it was a precise term which related to the specific problems they were facing. From December 1965 to January 1966 I was in Havana, attending the first Tri-Continental Conference of Asia, Africa and Latin America. Here, too, as I heard for myself, speaker after speaker described in the most detailed terms the activities and manifestations of neo-colonialism in his country. And here, too, as in Cairo, at the end of the conference the delegates endorsed a comprehensive resolution setting out the characteristics of neo-colonialism and the necessity to struggle against it.

The term neo-colonialism undoubtedly relates to a major political phenomenon of our time. As its name implies, it is in a sense colonialism in a new form. Many people, witnessing the

* *The Times*, March 21, 1964.

steady erosion since the end of the second world war of the old classic empires of direct colonial rule, have been inclined to accept the proposition that "imperialism is dead", that we have seen "the end of an Empire", and that "there are no more colonial problems". Certainly, colonialism has been dealt a heavy blow, but it is not yet dead. Over 70 territories, embracing more than 30 million people, remain as victims of direct colonial rule. But more important still, the developing countries of the "Third World" of Asia, Africa and Latin America, embracing the majority of mankind, have taken but the first major steps away from colonialism. Constitutional independence is theirs, but economic liberation has still to be won, and, until it is, political independence will never be complete and will always be in danger.

To understand neo-colonialism, therefore, we need to understand the essential features of twentieth-century colonialism, to examine why it is in decline, why neo-colonialism has emerged as a major factor of our time, how neo-colonialism functions, and how it can be defeated.

Such an examination would more than justify a lengthy volume, for there is enough experience and detailed information now available to enable one to make a comprehensive examination of this phenomenon. The present short book does not attempt such a task; it is rather a short introduction to the subject.

It is intended for the European and North American reader at least as much as for those in the "Third World"—for if the latter are the intended victims of neo-colonialism, it is from West European and North American Governments that this new threat comes. In the past two years there has been an obvious counter-offensive of neo-colonialism which has led to the assassination of popular national leaders, the overthrow of governments which failed to do imperialism's bidding, and the existence of serious tensions in a whole series of countries. The removal of this new menace must be of concern to progressive people everywhere. To overcome a threat one must understand it. It is the purpose of this short study to assist in bringing about such an understanding.

I

What is Colonialism?

The modern colonial system matured at the end of the nineteenth century as a consequence of the change from free competitive capitalism to monopoly capitalism or imperialism. Long before then territories in Africa, Asia, Australasia, and North and South America had been seized by the European powers—as military outposts, as trading centres, for the seizure of slaves, for the looting of gold and silver, and for white settlement. This was part of the process of the emergence of European capitalism.

> "The discovery of gold and silver in America, the extirpation, enslavement and entombment in mines of the aboriginal population, the beginning of the conquest and looting of the East Indies, the turning of Africa into a warren for the commercial hunting of black-skins, signalised the rosy dawn of the era of capitalist production."*

These activities, explained Marx, were "the chief momenta of primitive accumulation". On the basis of the wealth seized in this way, capitalism arose in Europe. The advance of industrial techniques in the nineteenth century, the growth of large-scale industry, and of concentrations of economic power in the hands of a relatively small number of major companies and banks led to a change in the pattern of relations between the European powers and the countries of Asia, Africa and Latin America. Expanding industries at home required increasing quantities of raw materials; the growth in the quantity of

* Marx, Karl: *Capital*, vol. 1, p. 751, London, 1954 edition. See also New York edition.

manufactured goods, including capital equipment, needed additional outlets to that of the home market; the possibilities of earning further profits at a still higher rate were at hand in the form of cheap land and cheap labour.

To ensure their full utilisation of these new possibilities, the European powers extended their grip on the whole world. Territories not yet in their possession were forcibly seized, sometimes by outright war and military action, sometimes in the ill-disguised form of "treaties" imposed on local rulers by a combination of force and plain deceit. Thus in Africa, following the Treaty of Berlin in 1885, which was attended by the major European powers together with the United States as a most interested observer, the whole African continent was divided up. By the beginning of the present century only Ethiopia and Liberia remained as sovereign African states. The same process went ahead in the Far East and South East Asia so that by 1900, of the main territories in this region only Japan, China, and Thailand remained outside the scope of direct colonial rule—though in the case of China the imperialists held stretches of Chinese territory and directly intervened in other ways.

To maintain their domination over their newly seized territories and ensure their utmost exploitation, the Western powers established full state power over them. "Belgian" Congo, "Portuguese" Guinea, "Spanish" Morocco, "Dutch" East Indies, "British" West Indies, "French" Indo-china, "German" East Africa—in giving these names to the lands they had taken, the European powers were openly proclaiming their intention to rule over them as subordinate parts of their own metropolitan states. By political, military, economic and ideological fetters, the European powers established their absolute power in the colonies.

The political essence of colonialism is the direct and overall subordination of one country to another on the basis of state power being in the hands of the dominating foreign power. Thus, European officials, sometimes accompanied by European-staffed governments and European (or mainly European) assemblies, were the constitutional powers in the colonies. These were protected by European armies, or sometimes armies of indigenous troops under European officers. The judges were Europeans and the laws were laid down by Europeans. The prisons were in the hands of Europeans, and so were the higher ranks in the civil administration. Education was controlled by Europeans, based on European history and culture, and limited to the general economic, social and political requirements of the colony-owning power. European missionaries introduced Christianity in competition with the existing religions of the local peoples. Press and other propaganda media were in the hands of Europeans.

This overall political power was directed to two main objectives—to keep the colonial people in political subjection; and to make possible the maximum exploitation of the people and the country's resources. This was clearly reflected in the laws and Government decrees. There was usually a whole array of laws to limit democracy—to outlaw strikes, ban or restrict trade unions, disallow or limit political parties, suppress criticism, close down local papers, banish or arrest political leaders, deny completely or severely restrict the franchise, and to permit only the most limited representation of the people in whatever nominated or elected assemblies were allowed.

These enactments were intended to tie the hands of the people so that they could not prevent their economic exploitation. This latter objective was facilitated even more directly by the European state power and legal system. Laws were enacted to lay down the lowest possible minimum wage, to impose a poll tax to compel peasants to take up wage labour, to introduce systems of forced labour, to sanctify systems of land tenure which robbed the peasant of his land, or left him with only a small plot of the poorest land, and sometimes to refuse him the right to grow the highest revenue-producing crops. It was to maintain this pattern of economic and political life that the colony-owning powers exercised state power.

In some cases, it is true, territories were seized not so much because of the wealth they contained or their economic potential, but as military bases which could help to safeguard imperialist interests in other more economically valuable territories. This was the case, for example, with Gibraltar, Malta, Cyprus and Aden.

But in an overall sense the economic motive was the dominant one. State power, direct foreign rule over the colonial peoples, was required not only to facilitate their exploitation but also to keep out possible rivals. Colonialism, wrote Lenin, was preferred by imperialism, because it alone "gives complete guarantees of success to the monopolies against all the risks of the struggle with competitors . . ." since "in the colonial market it is easier to eliminate competition, to maek sure of orders, to strengthen the necessary 'connections', etc., by monopolist methods (and sometimes it is the only possible way)".*

Colonialism enabled the imperialist powers to rob the colonial peoples in a variety of ways. They were able to secure cheap land, cheap labour, and cheap resources. They were free to impose a system of low-priced payments to peasant producers of export crops, to establish a monopoly-controlled market for the import of the manufactured goods of the colony-owning power (the goods often being manufactured from the raw materials of the colony itself), and secure a source of extra profit through investment. A consequence was the imposition of unfavourable terms of trade on the colonial peoples which obliged them to sell their labour power and their produce cheaply but to pay ever-mounting prices for the manufactured goods imported into their country by the imperialist traders.

The results on the economy of the colonial territories were almost catastrophic. The newly independent states of Africa and Asia inherit economies which are not merely undeveloped but *distorted*. Under colonialism a certain development took place, but one which resulted in a completely unbalanced economy, and in the impoverishment of the peoples. The

* Lenin, V. I.: *Imperialism—the Highest Stage of Capitalism*, pp. 100–103, London, 1948 edition. See also New York edition.

colonial countries were turned into bases for producing primary products—minerals and agricultural crops for export. Often the entire economy of a territory became based on one or two commodities—Ghana on cocoa, Gambia on ground-nuts, Zanzibar on cloves, Tanganyika on sisal and coffee, Malaya on rubber and tin, Ceylon on tea and rubber, Jamaica on sugar and bananas, Indonesia on rubber and tin, and so on. Crops, whether for food or for industrial purposes, were pro-duced either by lowly-paid agricultural wage labour on European-owned plantations, or by local peasant producers whose products were bought up cheaply by foreign trading monopolies. The minerals were almost everywhere produced by low-paid mineworkers employed in European-owned mines.

An illustration of the scale of exploitation and poverty of the colonial people is provided by Professor René Dumont who, when in Chad in 1950, calculated that "one hour of work for a cotton labourer would bring him about three-tenths of an inch of ordinary cotton cloth".* To earn three yards of cloth, this labourer would have to work over three hundred hours.

As a result of the form of colonial economy established by the imperialist countries, the big monopolies made a triple profit. They invested money in mines and plantations in Asia and Africa—and made fantastically high profits by exploiting the cheap wage labour. Secondly, monopoly trading firms such as the United Africa Company bought up cheaply raw materials produced by local peasants, and made huge profits from this source as well. Thirdly, foreign manufacturers made substan-tial profits by selling their goods in the colonies which were largely reserved for them as closed markets where the goods of other imperialist countries could not easily penetrate. Profits were also made from shipping and other services, as well as from banking and insurance operations. Thus, foreign mono-poly capitalism as a whole benefited from this system, while the colonial people were robbed as workers, as peasant producers, and as consumers. Often, in their role as consumers, the colonial

* Dumont, René: *False Start in Africa*, London, 1966, p. 40.

people were robbed by the shabbiest forms of swindling. Professor Dumont gives the following example:

"In December 1949, in the northern Congo (then Belgian), I picked up an alarm clock I wanted to buy in a little Greek shop. The proprietor quickly grabbed it out of my hands, saying: 'That's a treaty article, it only works for a few days.' But it was sold to the Congolese at the same price as good European clocks."*

In order to maintain this profitable system, the colonial powers prevented industrialisation in the colonies. They had no interest themselves in creating modern industry in their colonial territories since it was their aim to utilise the resources —raw materials and cheap labour—to feed their own industrial machines in Europe. And they had no intention of allowing the colonial peoples to build up industry in competition with their own. The consequence, which any visitor to Africa or Asia could witness for himself, was the virtual non-existence of industry and a dependence on the most primitive tools and equipment, and on every limb of the human body. For transport, the man-drawn rickshaw or the man-hauled boats of China. For carriage, the bamboo pole and baskets, or the basket carried on the head, or the goods carried on the head without even the basket. On building sites, no wheelbarrow, not even a hod; bricks carried by hand instead. In road-building, often the only equipment for breaking up a large stone was another stone. In agriculture, the man-drawn wooden plough and simple wooden hoe. For bringing down large trees, not even a two-handed saw but often a mere axe, which meant hours of tiring labour. Not everywhere, nor in every field of economic activity, did colonialism rely on such primitive equipment, but too often was this the case.

As for the absence of industry, one can take the example of Ghana. At the time of her winning independence, in 1957, she found she was exporting bauxite, importing aluminium pots and pans; exporting palm-oil, importing soap; exporting

* ibid, p. 40.

timber, importing furniture and paper; exporting hides, importing boots and shoes. The world's largest cocoa producer, she was exporting raw cocoa and having to import every bar of chocolate or tin of processed cocoa she required. She was even spending hundreds of thousands of pounds a year importing jute sacks into which to load her raw cocoa beans for export. Equally if not more incredible, a British firm owning lime plantations in Ghana actually expressed the juice from the fruit, and shipped the juice in bulk to Britain where it was bottled; the final product was exported back to Ghana where it was retailed at a high price in the local shops.*

Distortions to the economy of colonial territories were also to be seen in agriculture. The turning over of entire regions to the production of one or two cash crops meant a serious decline in the local growing of essential foodstuffs, so that there was that strange phenomenon of countries correctly classified as agrarian as regards the character of their economy, yet having to rely on imports for the simplest of food requirements, even in countries ideally suited to the growing of such crops or to the development of live-stock. Dr. Nkrumah has written:

"Under the British there was no poultry farming to speak of; there was no proper dairy farming, and the ordinary Gold Coast family never saw a glass of fresh milk in its life. There was no raising of beef cattle."†

Particularly striking is the example he gives of potato growing under colonial rule:

"During the war, British troops were stationed in the Gold Coast. Everyone knows that potatoes are to the British what bread is to the French. A meal is not complete without them. Under wartime conditions, shipping was severely restricted, and it looked as though the British soldiers would have to go without their potatoes. It had always been maintained that our climate was not suitable for growing them.

* Nkrumah, Kwame: *Africa Must Unite*, London, 1963, p. 27. See also New York edition.
† ibid., p. 29.

But the administration, moved at the thought of British servicemen being deprived of their staple food, began a 'grow potatoes' campaign. Before long, our hitherto 'unsuitable' climate was producing magnificent crops. Once the war was over, however, and normal shipping facilities were resumed, the Department of Agriculture changed its tune. Gold Coast potatoes, we were told, were unfit for human consumption. The result was that potatoes disappeared from our fields and once more figured among our imports".*

To complete the story one should add that during the period of Kwame Nkrumah's presidency Ghana once more began to grow potatoes for her own consumption.

A consequence of the colonial countries being maintained as raw materials appendages of western industry and commerce has been, as we have noted, that they had to sell cheap and buy dear. Statistics show that over long periods of time the prices of raw materials tend to fluctuate and often fall on the world market; and even when they rise it is only slowly compared with the steady increase in prices of manufactured goods which they have to buy, and still more in comparison with the rising prices of machinery. The United Nations Economic Bulletin for Africa (January 1961) states that the unit value of all agricultural products for export fell from 100 in 1953–1955 to 86 in 1959. In the past fifty years, while prices of foodstuffs in the world have risen by 130 per cent, and of mineral raw materials by some 90 per cent, those of manufactured goods have gone up by 300 per cent, and of machinery by 500 per cent. A graphic example of the loss caused to Africa through having to export her raw materials cheap and importing highly-priced goods manufactured from those same raw materials is provided by the case of wood. According to United Nations F.A.O. reports, in 1960 the difference in value between Africa's exports of logs and imports of wood products amounted to a loss to Africa of about £43 million. This is just for one item, wood, and over a period of only one year. When one

* ibid., p. 30.

takes into account all of Africa's main products, one can understand how considerable must have been the loss which has accumulated to Africa over the years of colonial rule. And the same, of course, goes for Asia.

How did this colonial system affect the people? For the overwhelming majority of them it meant extreme poverty, ill-health, bad housing, illiteracy, political tyranny and chronic hunger (politely known as malnutrition*) apart from sudden spells of absolute starvation. For the workers it meant bitter strikes for trade union rights and for even the smallest wage increase; and in such conflicts they had to be prepared to meet batons, bullets, prison and sometimes death. For most of the peasants it meant a permanent battle against poverty, a desperate struggle to scratch a living from a small piece of poor land, depending on the simplest of tools, and burdened with heavy rent, taxation, and usually interest payments to the money-lender, too. For the small stratum of educated, it meant constant frustration, a lack of opportunities to utilise their specialised skills and knowledge, and the frequent practice of racial discrimination which kept them out of jobs they were suited for, governments and employers in the colonies preferring that such positions should be staffed by Europeans. (It was not unknown for an Indian with a London degree in engineering to return home only to find employment as a garage attendant or some similar job far below his capabilities and qualifications.) Even for the indigenous capitalist class, itself usually very weak and confined mainly to trade, commerce, farming, money-lending, and some small-scale manufacturing,† it was difficult to flourish and expand in the face of the dominant positions in the economy held by foreign monopolies; and foreign control of banking meant limited credit facilities for local capitalists.

On the other hand, the bringing of vast areas of Asia and

* For a fuller treatment, see *Geography of Hunger*, Josué de Castro: London, 1952.

† In some cases, notably India, a richer and more powerful local bourgeoisie developed.

Africa into the orbit of imperialist control meant the introduction of the Western economy. Pre-capitalist forms of society, feudal and patriarchal, began to break up. Village industries and handicrafts succumbed to the flood of Western manufactures. Indigenous forms of subsistence agriculture began to be replaced by the large-scale growing of cash crops for export. The impoverishment of the peasantry compelled millions to take up wage labour. The growth of colonial administration and monopoly enterprises (large trading firms, managing agencies, shipping, banking, insurance and so on) created a demand for local clerks and administrative workers, and hence for a more educated élite. A modern trader, complete with lorries and clerical staff, began to emerge where once barter trade was more common. Thus, alongside the social classes of a pre-capitalist era—feudal landlords, peasants without rights, village craftsmen and artisans, scribes and priests, chiefs, sheikhs and rajahs—there began to appear the modern classes of wage workers and capitalists, accompanied by a stratum of professional, technical and service personnel holding modest posts in the colonial administration, providing N.C.O.'s in the armed forces, teachers in the primary schools, medical orderlies and male nurses in the hospitals, clerks in the offices, postal workers and shop assistants.

For practically everyone, apart from a privileged few, the colonial system became an object of hatred. All the progressive classes in colonial society felt frustrated. Their economic hardships, their limited possibilities of growth and improvement, the daily practice of racial discrimination, and the lack of political rights, all came to be seen as a natural consequence of foreign rule. Thus the struggle against colonialism, which became such a major phenomenon of the post-1945 era, was a struggle supported by the overwhelming majority of the people —workers and peasants, intellectuals and capitalists, small shopkeepers and traders, and even individual chiefs or members of royal families.*

* For fuller detail regarding the progressive role of some African chiefs see the present author's *Africa—The Roots of Revolt*, London, 1960, pp.

The participation of chiefs or members of royal families in the national liberation struggles was, however, an exception. Generally speaking, the indigenous ruling forces in the colonies, those who held the dominant economic and political positions under the European administrators and monopoly firms, were allies of the colonial system. This system, it should be appreciated, although depending mainly on the complete political and economic domination of the colony by the imperial power, could never have been maintained if not for the alliance which the imperialists were able to establish with a stratum of society within the colony.

In the 1920's there were only 7,400 Europeans in British West Africa amongst what was then a population of nearly twenty-three millions. In the whole of Asia, there were only 304,000 British in an aggregate population of 334 million.* In the Dacca and Chittagong divisions of Bengal, with a population of seventeen and a half millions, there were in 1907 only 21 British covenanted civil servants and 12 British police officers.† Thirty years later whole provinces in India were administered by a handful of British, assisted by Indian troops and police under the command of British officers. In Indo-China the French were a similarly exposed minority, as were the Dutch in the East Indies.

Clearly, despite their technical advantage in military terms, the Europeans could never have held on to their colonial possessions in the face of a united movement of awakened people. Thus it became a particular objective of colonial rule to keep the people divided, and to maintain them in a state of passive inertness, of obedience to existing rulers and acceptance of prevailing shibboleths, rules, traditions. Divide and rule, the playing off of one nationality, tribe, or religion against another, became an essential characteristic of colonialism,

266–73. Members of royal families in Asia who have thrown in their lot with the national independence movements include Prince Souphannouvong of Laos, and Prince Sihanouk of Cambodia.

* See Barraclough, G.: *An Introduction to Contemporary History*, London, 1964, p. 76.

† ibid.

especially on the part of successive British Governments which played off Tamil against Sinhalese in Ceylon, Hindu against Moslem in India, Jew against Arab in Palestine, Indian against Negro in British Guiana, Malay against Chinese in Malaya.

Economically, colonialism found its safest and most natural ally in the feudal landlords who, like the colonialists, had no interest in seeing an economic revolution in their country, were not concerned to carry through basic industrialisation, but were happy to support an economic system which gave them almost unlimited possibilities of exploiting their peasant tenants. Traders, who were often mere agents and middlemen for the foreign firms were also, as a rule, on the side of the colonial system which nurtured them and gave them the possibilities of enrichment.

Politically, the European powers preferred the forces of tradition rather than those who wanted to bring their countries into the twentieth century, to modernise their social and political life, to end backwardness and ignorance, to build modern towns and create modern industries. Rajahs, princes, sheikhs and chiefs were usually prepared to collaborate with the colonial powers on whom they depended for protection against the wrath of their own oppressed people; and on their side, the colonialists calculated that by bolstering the traditional rulers they would also ensure a continuation of traditional ideas, of religious superstitions and general obscurantism. In this way they hoped to cut off the colonial peoples from the enlightening and liberating ideas of freedom, democracy, national independence and, still more important, socialism, which, since the Russian revolution of 1917, became a veritable nightmare to every colonial administrator in the third world.*

In a sense, therefore, it can be said that while colonialism meant the direct political and economic domination of one country by another, on the basis of state power being in the

* In my personal contacts with British officials in Asia in the 1930's—with passport officials, police inspectors, prison wardens and so on—I could not help noticing their obsessive fears about communism.

hands of the colonial power, it was never solely a question of foreign rule, but rather that of foreign rule allied with certain economic and political strata of the indigenous people which had an interest in supporting colonialism. Thus colonial rule was in reality an alliance—an alliance between the occupying power and the internal forces of conservatism and tradition.

Yet, as the twentieth century continued, the requirements of colonial rule itself as well as the new economic and administrative needs arising from technical advance made it necessary for the colonial powers, to one degree or another, to create and attract other forces which could play a part in making it possible for the colonial system to function. Thus there arose in a number of territories, especially where there was no heavy European settlement, a stratum of educated individuals drawn from the indigenous populations, a stratum moreover, which was reared in the traditions of the colony-owning power and, apart from a difference in the colour of skin, was often virtually a carbon copy of the original.

In India, the steps to encourage the growth of an educated, westernised élite were taken as early as the nineteenth century, and the introduction of the Morley-Minto reforms in 1909 was in fact based on the existence already of "a class of persons, Indian in blood and colour, but English in taste, in opinion, in morals, and in intellect,"* on whose support Britain anticipated it could rely. The new élite which began to emerge in the colonies, as Mansur† correctly points out, was "not a new élite created by the colonial impact out of a diversified society at random" but "a part of the traditional élite, whether political or cultural". Some members of this élite were later to play a prominent part in the national independence movements, but many passively accepted the colonial system; and the colonial powers, in fostering them, generally regarded them as a secondary support to their main ally, the

* *New Cambridge Modern History*, vol. xii, p. 215. Cited in Barraclough, op. cit.
† Mansur, Fatma: *Process of Independence*, London, 1962, p. 65.

25

traditional rulers and landlords connected with the pre-capitalist economic forms, mainly feudal.

In subsequent years, too, after the winning of independence, the Western-trained élite were to be regarded by the imperialist powers as potential allies in their effort to maintain a Western "presence" in the Third World. Thus Sir Hugh Foot (now Lord Caradon) has written of those political figures in Asia and Africa who have been "trained in the traditions of the British Civil Service; their outlook and methods and instincts come from that training . . . men like Quaison-Sackey of Ghana, Adebo of Nigeria, and Adeel of the Sudan, are English not only in their training but also in their attitude to public affairs".*

No doubt in the former French-occupied territories in Africa and Asia too, political figures can be found whom their backers in France would regard as "French" both in their training and in their attitude to public affairs.

It was because colonialism had an internal ally, at first mainly feudal and pre-capitalist with the support of compradore traders,† but later supplemented by sections of the new élite, that the anti-colonial revolution had to be spearheaded increasingly not only against the foreign power which ruled over the colony but equally against those domestic social, economic and political forces which, by their collaboration with the occupying power both directly and indirectly, had made it possible for the colonial system to be maintained. Naturally, the independence struggle has not always been thoroughgoing nor at all times conducted with a full understanding of the character of the internal support on which colonialism relied. Somtimes, the national liberation movement was at a lower stage of development, was not conscious of colonialism's internal ally, and was concerned only with the foreign power. Nevertheless, in all cases, the requirements of complete national liberation make it necessary for the inde-

* "Teaching the Nations How to Live": *The Observer Weekend Review*, February 3, 1963. The arrogance of the title of this article speaks for itself.
† Traders who act mainly as agents for foreign monopolies.

pendence struggle to combine the overthrow of foreign political rule and foreign economic domination with the defeat of those traditional domestic forces, economic and political, which stand in the way of democracy and revolutionary change. In other words, the anti-colonial struggle, to be complete, has to become a political, social and economic revolution, one that destroys both imperialism and feudalism or other pre-capitalist formations, and makes possible the full democratic participation of the people in running the affairs of the new state so that they can refashion their lives and ensure the building of a modern and prosperous society.

2

Why Neo-Colonialism?

Direct colonial rule was the most effective form for the imperialist powers because it gave them unfettered control over the man-power and resources of the major part of the world. It made it possible, too, for each imperialist power to keep out rivals from "its" territories and prevent the intrusion of competing monopoly firms; and it facilitated the maintenance of troops and bases on the spot to defend the economic interests of the Western powers. To cap it all, colonial rule made it possible to burden the colonial people themselves with paying for the very troops which held them down.

But today old-style colonialism is vanishing. In 1919, over 1,200 million people out of a world population of 1,800 million, that is to say almost 70 per cent, were in colonies, semi-colonies or dominions. By 1966 direct colonial rule had disappeared over most of Asia, Africa and the Caribbean. Only some thirty million people (mainly in southern Africa, together with a number of small islands and territories scattered throughout the world), amounting to considerably less than one per cent of mankind, remain under European or American rule.

Thus, in terms of human history, the modern colonial system which came into being at the end of the last century has been only a passing phenomenon. "Never before in the whole of human history had so revolutionary a reversal occurred with such rapidity."* And the reason is not far to seek. The decline of direct colonial rule has coincided with the expansion of socialism. In 1914 the big imperialist powers dominated the

* Barraclough, G.: op. cit., p. 148.

whole world. In 1917 they lost one sixth of the earth's surface and about ten per cent of its population. The Russian revolution of October 1917 ushered in a new world epoch, the epoch of socialism. The victory of the Russian workers and peasants over the Tsar at the same time liberated thirty-three millions of non-Russian peoples from the former "prison-house of nations". This had a profound effect on the oppressed peoples throughout the colonial and semi-colonial world.

"The October Revolution" wrote Stalin in 1918, "is the first revolution in world history to break the age-long sleep of the labouring masses of the oppressed peoples of the East and to draw them into the fight against world imperialism."*

"The salvoes of the October Revolution brought us Marxism-Leninism" confirmed Mao Tse-tung.†

"The cause for which revolutionary Mexico and newly-emancipated Russia are fighting is the common cause of all mankind" declared Mexico's revolutionary peasant leader, Emiliano Zapata, a few months after the October Revolution.‡

From the very beginning, the young socialist state took a number of steps to assist and co-operate with neighbouring countries striving to throw off foreign rule. Thus, it was the first to recognise the independence of Afghanistan (1919), Turkey (1920), and Mongolia (1921). It concluded treaties based on equality and respect for mutual interests with Turkey, Iran and Afghanistan (1921), China (1924), and Yemen (1928). Its publication of the tsarist government's secret treaties, and especially the Sykes-Picot documents exposing Anglo-French intrigues over Palestine, further undermined the prestige and positions of the colonial powers, as did its open renunciation of concessions which tsarist governments had forced from other states, as in the case of China. It also gave direct help to people engaged in military struggles against

---

* Stalin, J. V.: *The October Revolution and the National Question*, Pravda, November 6 and 19, 1918; Works, vol. 4, 1953, p. 167.

† Mao Tse-tung: *On the People's Democratic Dictatorship*, June 30, 1949; Selected Works, vol. IV (Peking edition, 1961) p. 413.

‡ See Stepanov, L.: *International Affairs* (Moscow), No. 10, 1966, p. 56.

domestic and foreign reaction; it sent military advisors to assist Dr. Sun Yat-sen in China and Kemal Ataturk in Turkey, and troops to help the people of Mongolia. All this, too, had a profound effect on the national liberation movements.

Throughout Asia one can trace the sudden rise of the national liberation movements after 1917. The year 1919 saw the March 1 uprising in Korea, the historic "Fourth of May" movement in China, the formation of the Ceylon National Congress, and the rapid transformation of the national movement of Sarekat Islam in Indonesia to a mass organisation of two and a half million members.* In India, 1919 was a year of unprecedented unrest, of widespread strikes and demonstrations, which were countered by the British authorities with extraordinary ferocity, including the appalling atrocity at Amritsar when troops under General Dyer fired 1,600 rounds of ammunition into an unarmed crowd in an enclosed place without exit, killing (according to official figures) 379 and leaving 1,200 wounded. In Burma, 1920 witnessed the big "December Boycott" movement.†

In Africa, too, new voices were being heard, and these found partial expression at the first Pan-African Congress in 1919. In the same year the Wafd Party was formed in Egypt and the Destour Party in Tunisia. In 1920 the West African Congress came into being; in 1921 the South African Communist Party was born. The same year saw the big movement of protest and strikes in Kenya, and the commencement of the Rif rebellion led by Abdelkrim in Morocco.

The ensuing twenty-five years saw ever-mounting struggles for national independence throughout Africa and Asia, yet world imperialism was still the dominant force and only a few colonies were able, in this period, to break the fetters of imperialist rule. By the end of the second world war, however, a major shift in world relations began to make itself felt. In Eastern Europe and in Asia a series of countries overthrew

---

* Kahin, G. M.: *Nationalism and Revolution in Indonesia*, Ithaca, 1952, pp. 65/6. Cited in Barraclough, op. cit.

† Tinker, Hugh: *South Asia*, London, 1966, p. 203.

tyranny and outmoded economic systems and set out on the road to socialism. The liberation of China, in 1949, brought the total of those who had escaped completely from exploitation by the big imperialist monopoly firms to about one thousand million people, a third of mankind.

This total shift in world relations could not but have a most profound effect on the world, and weaken still further the capacity of the Western powers to hold on to their colonies.

At the same time, with the emergence of modern class forces in the colonial countries—national bourgeoisie, intelligentsia and working class—the people's liberation movements themselves had grown, and were dealing ever more powerful blows against their oppressors. In 1945 national independence uprisings took place in Vietnam and Indonesia, and a People's Republic was proclaimed in Korea. In 1946, India was shaken by the naval mutiny which compelled Britain to concede independence a year later. In 1947 the people of Madagascar rose in revolt. Burma became independent in 1948. China's liberation war was crowned with success in 1949. In 1950, the people of Ghana launched their "Positive Action Campaign". In 1952, the patriotic officers overthrew King Farouk in Egypt, and the same year a State of Emergency was declared in Kenya, to be followed by four years of armed struggle. In 1953, the People's Progressive Party under Dr. Cheddi Jagan swept into victory in the elections that year in British Guiana. In 1954 the French were defeated at Dien Bien Phu; and the Algerians began their war against French rule. Then followed the Suez crisis of 1956, and the struggles in Tunisia and Morocco culminating in the independence of those two countries in 1956; the winning of independence by Ghana in 1957, and by Guinea in 1958; the overthrow of Nuri al-Said in Iraq in 1958, and of Batista in Cuba in 1959. Each of these actions weakened imperialism as a world force and, in combination with the socialist camp, represented an alliance which could no longer be crushed.

In the metropolitan countries, too, the movement of the people against colonialism grew considerably after 1945, as expressed by the big movements in France against the wars in Algeria and Vietnam, and the protests in Britain against the repression in Kenya in the 1950's, in solidarity with the African miners on the Zambian Copper Belt in 1952, in the huge movement in 1956 at the time of the Suez crisis, and more recently against apartheid in South Africa, and against the sell-out to Smith in Southern Rhodesia. All these forms of public protest have hampered imperialism, made it more difficult for it to justify the continuation of colonial rule, and facilitated the struggles of the peoples for independence. The present world-wide movement of protest over the U.S. war in Vietnam is a further example of this important development.

Thus a coming together of three main political forces on the international scene—the socialist countries, the national liberation movements themselves, and the working class, democratic and peace movements in the metropolitan countries—has been strong enough to compel the imperialists to retreat and therefore has spelt the doom of the system of direct colonial rule. The adoption of the United Nations Resolution on the Ending of Colonialism is an expression of this changed situation in the world.

The compulsion on imperialism to abandon almost everywhere its old forms of direct colonial rule, political domination and economic exploitation, with the latter facilitated and buttressed by colonial legislation made possible by the exercise of state power, has meant a real retreat on the part of the Western powers. And the retreat, in its turn, has resulted in these powers seeking for new forms through which they can maintain the essentials of their economic domination and still wield political influence.

The fact that direct colonial rule has been ended since 1945 in some sixty countries of Asia, Africa and the Caribbean, (inhabited by 1,250 million people, one third of mankind), should not blind us to the intensity of the struggle which the colonial peoples usually had to wage in order to achieve independent statehood. The picture sometimes presented of an orderly, generous abandonment of colonial rule by the Western powers, is nowhere confirmed by the facts. In fact, these powers did everything possible after 1945 to regain their positions in Asia which they had lost to Japan during the war. Not yet confronted by the combined strength of a world-wide socialist camp, aware that the national liberation movements had not yet reached their full stature, and conscious of their monopoly at that time of the atom bomb, the imperialist states strove to stamp out the flames of national resurgence in Asia where the peoples were striking the first major blows against the colonial system. The war had been a stern test of this system. All the imperialist powers—the British in Burma and Malaya, the French in Indochina, the Dutch in Indonesia, as well as the Americans in the Philippines—had proved themselves incapable of defending the peoples against fascism, and unwilling to arm the people to defend themselves. Furthermore, they had been driven out of their strongholds by an Asian power, Japan, and this meant a further weakening of the prestige of the West in Asia.

ATTEMPTED RECONQUEST IN ASIA

As the war ended, the Western powers moved quickly to try to re-establish their power. There was little talk at this stage of "granting independence", despite the Atlantic Charter. In Indochina, the collapse of the Japanese in 1945 was the signal for the people's uprising and the quick establishment of their independent power in the form of the Democratic Republic of Vietnam whose writ ran the length and breadth of Vietnam, north and south, including Hanoi and Saigon.

"Thus the Republic of Vietnam came into being, while the occupying Japanese army stood by, awaiting its fate, and thousands of unmolested but unarmed Frenchmen looked helplessly on. The new regime took swift hold. In the cities and the countryside there was order. Markets thrived, utilities and public services continued to function. In government bureaux Annamites set about the exciting business of creating a government of their own. There were scarcely any incidents. In all the month of August, by subsequent French acknowledgement, only one Frenchman was killed in a street clash. The Vietnam government opened wide the prison gates. Thousands of political prisoners came blinking into the light from the sordid dungeons of Saigon and Hue and Hanoi and other cities. . . . The Annamites believed that what they had won for themselves, the victorious Allies would never take away."*

Shortly afterwards, the first British representatives arrived in Saigon. Under the terms of agreements reached between the war-time allies, Britain was acknowledged as being responsible in the region of all south-eastern Asia for enforcing surrender terms on the Japanese and in assisting in "restoring law and order". Britain's interpretation of "restoring law and order" proved to be the imposition, where it was possible, of the former colonial regimes which had collapsed so rapidly in the face of the Japanese attack.

In Vietnam, the British refused to treat directly with the new Government which the people had set up. It refused to acknowledge their letters, and ignored their offer of help to disarm the Japanese troops. On the contrary the British authorities in Saigon ordered the Japanese to keep their troops in full war kit; martial law was declared; the French troops which had been interned by the Japanese were rearmed; Vietnamese papers were suppressed; orders were given to disband the people's militia and police; and Vietnamese authorities were evicted from key buildings in Saigon. All these measures were the prelude to a coup d'état on September 23, 1945, when the French troops seized key buildings in Saigon, arrested hundreds of prisoners and killed those who resisted. In the following weeks, with British and French troop reinforcements, and aided even by the Japanese troops (the British official spokesman on October 18, 1945, thanking the Japanese commander, General Terauchi, "with highest praise", for his

* Isaacs, Harold R.: *No Peace For Asia*, 1947. (Quoted in the Penguin Special, *Vietnam*, 1966.)

co-operation), the colonial powers strove to re-establish French rule in Vietnam. Describing the events of 1945 in south Vietnam, Harold R. Isaacs wrote: "By grace of the British, and with the aid of the Japanese, the French had regained a toehold in Indochina . . ."*

With that toehold, the French tried to reconquer Vietnam. By 1954, culminating in their disastrous defeat at Dien Bien Phu, the French had been defeated; the attempt to regain their colonial territory had failed. Henceforward it was to be the American rulers who would try to bring Vietnam under their control.

Vietnam showed that the colonial powers were determined to try to recover their colonial territories; and, above all, to prevent their passing into the hands of Governments led by Communists and other anti-imperialist forces.

The experience of Indonesia after 1945 paralleled that of Vietnam. There, too, on August 17, 1945, the people took over from the Japanese and set up their own Republic. There, too, the 80,000 Japanese troops, still armed, were ordered by the commander of the British forces in South East Asia to keep "law and order" until Allied troops arrived. In bitter fighting with the Japanese, the Indonesian people established their control, and within a few months the Indonesian Republic became a reality. Shortly after the Japanese capitulation the Dutch government started preparations to re-establish its rule in Indonesia. With the help of the British forces, and aided by the Japanese troops whom the British released and armed once again,† the Dutch invaded in full force. Dutch troops landed at several points in Java and other islands. Djakarta was captured in West Java, and an invasion by land, sea and air was launched at Sourabaja in East Java. For the next three and a half years, the people of Indonesia had to struggle against the

* Isaacs, Harold R.: op. cit.

† This was indicated in the statement made by Mr. Noel Baker, Minister of State, December 11, 1945. The *Daily Express* (December 22, 1945) reported that Japanese troops were being armed in Sumatra with "the latest Mark 69 tanks".

Dutch forces, arms in hand, until the former colonial masters were compelled to retreat and accept the fact of Indonesian independence and the reality of the Republic.*

What the French tried to do in Indochina, and the Dutch in Indonesia, the British did, more successfully, in Malaya. In August 1945, the Malayan People's Anti-Japanese Army, which had heroically taken up arms after the ignominious collapse of the British at Singapore, and had fought throughout the war, took over from the Japanese.

Through their political organisation, the Malayan People's Anti-Japanese Union, the people established control in all the main centres. It was not until September that the first British units arrived. They insisted on the disarming of the forces of the people's army and refused to recognise the governmental authority of the union. Provocations led to clashes, until in 1948 the wholesale attack on the trade unions and other democratic organisations whose leaders were arrested or shot down, compelled the active members to flee to the countryside to take up armed struggle once again for the liberation of their territory. Several years of guerrilla warfare ensued, in which Malayan patriots, several of whom had been decorated by Lord Mountbatten for their bravery, and had marched in the 1945 Victory Parade in the Mall, in London, were brutally murdered.†

It was not until 1957 that Malaya was allowed constitutional independence—and then only after the decline of the guerrilla forces had made it possible for Britain to hand over power to an alliance of feudal and compradore trading interests which were more likely to prove co-operative.

* This was not the end of attempts to re-establish imperialist domination in Indonesia. In the ensuing years there were plots and rebellions against the Republic. A major blow was the military coup of October 1965 in which several hundred thousand Indonesian Communists and other democratic and patriotic people were massacred.

† Such was the case with the outstanding patriot and revolutionary leader, Liew Yau. For more details of the post-1945 struggle in Malaya see Woddis, Jack: *Stop the War in Malaya*, London, 1950; and Dutt, R. P.: *The Crisis of Britain and the British Empire*, London, 1953, pp. 101–114.

Throughout Asia the story was the same. Everywhere the colonial powers, aided by the United States (which was simultaneously playing its own game in order to step into the shoes of the other colonial powers), strove to keep the people down. Where they thought it possible, they tried to re-establish the old colonial system, as in Vietnam, Indonesia and Malaya. In other Asian territories, too, they endeavoured to retain, in varied and most appropriate forms, the essence of their power. In Burma, Britain was compelled to grant independence in January 1948—but only after the anti-imperialist leader, Aung San, and his key ministers had been assassinated by pro-Western henchmen, thus paving the way for the conceding of independence to a government more likely to prove co-operative with British monopoly interests.

In Korea, Japan, as a defeated power, was unable to re-establish her rule. Moreover, the temporary Soviet occupation in the North, and the strength of the national liberation movement led by Kim Il Sung put a brake on imperialist plans. But here, too, as in Vietnam, Indonesia and Malaya, the Western powers tried to brush aside the Korean people's own patriotic bodies and institutions and set up a regime under their control. Under the war-time agreements for the Japanese surrender, Korea was temporarily divided at the 38th parallel. Japan surrendered on August 14, 1945, and the Soviet troops, as arranged for by the surrender agreement, moved south to the 38th parallel.* The Japanese forces fled in the face of the advancing Russians, anticipating a warmer welcome from the American forces which landed in south Korea on September 8, 1945, nearly a month after the surrender. The late Professor McCune described the contrast in these words:

"The atmosphere between the Japanese and the occupying forces in the north was one of enmity. In the south the

* In fact, Soviet troops had already begun the liberation of Korea prior to the Japanese surrender, and on the surrender date were already in north-east Korea and rapidly advancing to the south.

37

Japanese assumed an attitude of guileless co-operation toward the occupying authorities."*

The Soviet authorities in Korea, explains Professor McCune, placed reliance on the local people's committees set up by the Koreans. On September 6, 1945, two days before the arrival of the American troops, a national congress was held in Seoul (in the south), "attended by representatives from all parts of Korea". This congress was initiated by Korean leaders, including many patriots released from Japanese prisons in Korea after the surrender. An outstanding liberal leader of these forces was Lyuh Woonhyung. The congress proclaimed the People's Republic of Korea on September 6. "When American forces arrived in South Korea on September 8, the People's Republic offered its services to the American command, but was given a cold shoulder."† The American General Hodge attempted at first to retain the existing Japanese administration, but was compelled by public protest to drop the idea.‡ At the same time, the Americans backed the right-wing "Provisional Government" in exile, and brought back its leader, Syngman Rhee, who had been living for years in the United States. There was no doubt of the popular support for the People's Republic. The *Christian Science Monitor's* representative reported on January 3, 1946, that "the so-called People's Republic . . . enjoys far more support than any other single political grouping." But the American authorities were not interested in which political grouping was most representative of the people. It was determined to establish its own power in the south (and was later to attempt to take over the north as well). Lyuh Woonhyung was assassinated, the democratic movement in the south suppressed, and an American puppet government under the dictator Syngman Rhee installed against the wishes of the Korean people.

In the Philippines, too, American armed might ensured that the democratic forces of the people and their liberation move-

* McCune, George M.: *Korea Today*, Cambridge, Mass., 1950, p. 45.
† McCune, George M.: ibid. p. 47.
‡ Sarafan, Bertram D.: *Far Eastern Survey*, November 1946, p. 350.

ment which had fought the Japanese occupation forces, were forced into retreat and more conservative strata hoisted into power. The Philippine people's anti-Japanese army was known as the Hukbalahap. By September 1944 it had an effective armed strength of 10,000 men, a reserve of 40,000, and a mass base of no less than 500,000. So effective was this force that when the U.S. troops landed, they found many areas cleared of the Japanese, and were thus enabled to make a very rapid advance. General Decker, chief-of-staff of the U.S. Sixth Army, publicly admitted: "The Hukbalahap is one of the best fighting units I have ever known."*

On the basis of the Philippine Independence Act passed by the U.S. Congress in 1934, the Philippines was declared independent on July 4, 1946. In preparation for this step, the U.S. authorities took all the necessary measures to crush the forces of the left, and to retain their economic and political control. The main instrument for this was the Bell Trade Act of April 1946. Under this Act the Philippines had to agree to free trade with the United States—which meant American dumping, and the removal of all protection from the Philippines' own small-scale industry—the pegging of the currency to the U.S. dollar, and the fixing of quotas for exports to the U.S. while none were laid down for U.S. exports to the Philippines. Furthermore, the Philippine Constitution was amended to grant Americans "parity" with Filipinos in developing natural resources and operating public utilities. This "parity" between the powerful American monopolies and the relatively weak Filipino companies resulted in massive American investment in the islands' key resources and enterprises.

At the same time, the U.S. State Department and the Pentagon, by a combination of dollars and military repression, helped the war-time puppet, Manuel Roxas, to win the presidential elections. A Bases Agreement in 1947 granted the U.S. 22 bases on a rent-free 99 year lease. Now began the attack on the people's organisations. The National Peasants' Union, the

* Quoted in *U.S. and the Philippines*, Labour Research Association, New York, 1958, p. 20.

Huks, and the Communist Party were outlawed. Three union leaders were killed, and an attack launched against the people and their People's Liberation Army (which replaced the war-time Hukbalahap). Mr. Clark Lee, International News Service correspondent, describing the offensive against the people, reported that Roxas "backed by the 90,000 American troops in the Philippines . . . directed his American-armed and trained constabulary forces to open civil war against the small farmers living on the fertile plains north of Manila. Instead of initiating land reforms that would break up the huge holdings of the Catholic Church and of his Spanish-Filipino friends, Roxas turned loose tanks, armoured cars, bazookas and machine-guns against the men and women who sought to put an end to the tenant-farmer system and to win for their chil-dren a place in the new world for which so many Filipinos died."* Bitter, bloody struggle was to ensue in the Philippines for several years before the United States could feel confident that it had established a certain precarious stability there.

In India, the British rulers hoped after 1945 to maintain their full colonial rule, but the widespread strikes and the powerful naval mutiny of 1946, when the sailors hoisted the united flags of the Indian National Congress, the Muslim League, and the Communist Party, showed that that great country of nearly 500 million people was on the verge of a revolution. British arms were insufficient to hold down such a powerful force rising in revolt. It was to take 130,000 armed men to defeat a few thousand guerillas in Malaya, a country of less than five million; clearly a war to maintain colonial rule in India was utterly out of the question. The establishment of Indian independence in 1947 was not a generous act by Bri-tain, but the only choice open to her. In boasting about this concession, the British Government was only making a virtue out of a necessity.†

* Lee, Clark: *One Last Look Around*, New York, 1947, p. 256.

† That Britain had no choice was, in fact, admitted by official spokesmen, notably Sir Stafford Cripps, in the Parliamentary debate, March 5, 1947. For details see Dutt, R. P.: op. cit., pp. 191/2.

A major attempt by the Western powers to re-establish imperialist control in Asia after the war was made in semi-colonial China. The United States was determined to prevent the Chinese people, under the leadership of its Communist Party, from taking over power in the most heavily populated country in the world. Arms and money poured into China from the United States to assist the Chiang Kai-shek regime and to halt the advancing armies of liberation. According to the information provided in the U.S. State Department White Paper, *United States Relations with China*, issued on August 5, 1949, the total value of U.S. aid to Chiang Kai-shek from the time of the commencement of the war against Japan until 1948 was more than 4,500 million dollars. An estimate given by the American Committee for a Democratic Far Eastern Policy in 1948 sets the figure for the period between V-J Day (1945) and February 1948 as high as 5,000 million dollars, and contrasts with this a figure of 1,500 million dollars of supplies to China for the entire war against Japan. The millions of dollars which America spent to save Chiang Kai-shek and establish U.S. power in China was, however, in vain; 1949 was not 1927, when it had been possible to massacre the workers of Shanghai and Canton, and to force the Chinese Revolution to retreat to the countryside. Now the world was different; a powerful socialist camp was emerging; national liberation movements throughout the world had advanced; popular opinion in the West was opposed to the U.S. intervention in China; and the Chinese national liberation movement itself had become irresistibly strong. As a result of these developments, the U.S. was unable to prevent the victory of the Chinese revolution.

In Africa, all movements and actions of an anti-colonial character were restricted or forcibly suppressed in the first decade or more after 1945. The people's rebellion in Madagascar in 1947 was put down with ferocity, and thousands were slaughtered by the French troops. In 1948, demonstrating ex-servicemen in Ghana were shot down, as were striking coal miners in Enugu, Nigeria, in 1949. In the Cameroons and Kenya, repression against the liberation forces compelled thousands to take up arms. Throughout Africa, in that period, it was clear that the colonial powers had no intention of quitting. Even as late as 1954, the people of Algeria were forced into armed struggle, and bitter conflict against the French authorities was waged in Tunisia and Morocco as well; two years later came the assault in Egypt.

It has been necessary to outline in some detail the events in Asia and Africa after 1945 in order to explain the background to the emergence of neo-colonialism. It has often been asserted that neo-colonialism is a retreat on the part of imperialism, an abandonment of direct colonial rule and the conceding of political independence. This is partly true, but if one examines the history of colonial struggle and imperialist tactics in the post-1945 period, then it is clear that an essential element of neo-colonialism is counter-revolution.

It was not so much a question of the formal granting of independence which worried the imperialists—though even that was a retreat which they would have preferred not to undertake; rather it was a determination to prevent, at all costs, the emergence of independent governments in Asia and Africa that would represent the most consistent anti-imperialist forces, and especially the workers and peasants. Where such forces were led by Communists, the counter-revolution was waged especially ferociously. Thus, in the post-1945 period, and particularly in Asia where the national liberation movement had reached the highest stage, the first steps taken by the imperialists were intended to crush by brute force, by military action, the assassination of popular leaders, the outlawing of mass organisations, and so on, the left wing of the national liberation movements and their leaderships.* At all costs, the workers and peasants must not be allowed to come to power.

* The same imperialist policy was pursued in Latin America after 1945. The Brazilian Communist Party, with 800,000 votes in the 1946 elections, was outlawed in 1947. In that same year, the Chilean Communist Ministers were forced out of the Popular Front Government of Chile, the Communist Party was banned, and thousands arrested. In Venezuela, the liberal government of Gallegos was overthrown by a coup in November 1948, and the Communist Party was outlawed. And so it went on right across the con-

Once this danger had been averted, the imperialists sought to make an accommodation which would partially satisfy the national aspirations of the people while protecting at the same time imperialist economic interests and assisting their general political and strategic aims. Only on such a basis was it possible to advance to the next phase of the neo-colonialist tactic. Where the colonial powers were unable to prevent the coming to power of governments representing the workers and peasants, as in China, North Korea and North Vietnam (and ten to fifteen years later in Cuba), the successful operation of neo-colonialism proved impossible.

From what has been said above, it is evident that as far as motives were concerned, *the Western powers had every intention after 1945 of re-establishing the essential pattern of colonial rule which had existed in Asia and Africa prior to the war. And for more than a decade they strove to that end. It was only the changed world situation and the strength of the national liberation movements themselves which compelled colonialism to retreat.*

But if imperialism has been forced to surrender its direct rule over most of the former colonial territories, it has not done this readily. Where it is still able or where it considers that its interests demand it, it strives to hold on to absolute rule, as the Portuguese do in Angola, Mozambique and "Portuguese" Guinea, or the British in Aden and Hong Kong. In a more indirect way, too, making use of local white minorities, the Western powers are doing everything possible to prevent the African people in Southern Rhodesia, South Africa and South West Africa assuming their rightful power in their own homelands.

The experience of the past two decades shows that the colonial powers only retreat when they are pushed out, or where they decide that their direct control is no longer required. Where they deem it necessary for their interests, they are quite

tinent. Military coups against liberal governments, the assassination of labour leaders, mass arrests, the outlawing of Communist Parties, and the general suppression of democratic rights. This was American imperialism's reply in Latin America to the post-war upsurge of the people's movements.

prepared to use the utmost military force to hold on to their colonial possessions.

But life presses on. The world is no longer under their domination; and despite what they desire or what they strive to do, the area of classical colonial rule is shrinking year after year and is fated to disappear entirely long before the end of this century.

It is in this new situation of dying colonialism, that neo-colonialism appears as a major phenomenon in the world. It is a weakness of the older imperialist powers that they have been compelled to turn from direct colonial rule to the indirect form of neo-colonialism. United States imperialism has generally supported the colonial powers in their efforts to re-establish their colonial empires after the second world war, but, at the same time, has quickly manoeuvred to ensure its presence and influence and investments whenever it was clear that direct colonial rule was on its way out. Thus, by 1954, the United States was providing no less than 80 per cent of the expenses needed by the French in their war to regain control of Vietnam. But when the French gave in, it was the United States which inherited the "burden" and which is now attempting to maintain its own neo-colonialist base in South Vietnam.

If the turn from direct colonial rule to the indirect form, neo-colonialism, is an expression of the weakness of imperialism, then it is also true that the ability of the imperialist powers to utilise neo-colonialist methods with some degree of temporary success in a number of countries is a sign of the insufficient strength and maturity of the national liberation movements in such countries, as well as of the insufficient unity amongst the forces arrayed against imperialism on a world scale. The balance of world forces today, and the strength of the national liberation movements in the different territories, are strong enough to force imperialism generally to retreat but not yet to overcome it utterly.

In those territories such as Cuba, or North Vietnam, where working class power has been established, it has been possible to dig up the roots of imperialism and prevent the operation of neo-colonialism. In contrast, in Brazil and Indonesia, both much more powerful states than the two continental parallels given above, the ability of indigenous feudal and reactionary capitalist classes to occupy key political positions and control important sectors of the economy, combined with the relative weakness and lack of unity of the national liberation forces, notwithstanding powerful Communist Parties in both cases, has led to temporary successes for neo-colonialism. Thus it is clear that a further strengthening and firmer cohesion of the national liberation forces within each particular country, together with the further advance and greater unity of all anti-imperialist forces on a world scale, is required if neo-colonialism is to be defeated and the peoples are to win their complete liberation.

EARLIER FORMS OF NEO-COLONIALISM

In a certain sense, neo-colonialism is not an entirely new phenomenon. Lenin pointed out that "finance capital is such a great, it may be said, such a decisive force in all economic and international relations, that it is capable of subordinating to itself, and actually does subordinate to itself, even states enjoying complete political independence."* Lenin subsequently emphasised the necessity "to explain to and expose among the broadest masses of the toilers of all countries, and particularly of backward countries, the deception systematically practised by the imperialists in creating, under the guise of politically independent states, states which are wholly dependent upon them economically, financially and militarily."†

For years Britain exercised her power in decisive areas of the Middle East without, in the main, wielding direct colonial rule. Egypt (declared independent in 1922), Iraq (declared independent in 1927), Iran (never reduced to actual colonial

* Lenin, V. I.: *Imperialism—The Highest Stage of Capitalism*, 1916, London, 1948 edition, pp. 99-100. See also New York edition.

† Lenin, V. I.: *Draft Theses on the National and Colonial Question*, June 1920. *Collected Works*, Vol. 31 pp 144-151.

status), Jordan (proclaimed independent in 1946), and other territories in this region were part of the "British sphere of influence", although they enjoyed the constitutional status of independent states. Independence, in reality, was restricted not only by the fact of British economic domination, but by the military and political fetters placed on these independent states. British troops remained in the Canal Zone, and British bases in Iraq. Behind King Faud and King Feisal stood Britain, as it was later to stand behind King Hussein.

China, too, though exercising nominal independence, was up to the time of her liberation in 1949 the victim of indirect forms of domination by imperialism. At first China was a semi-colony of imperialism as a whole. Britain, the United States, France, Germany, Italy, and Japan, all had their investments in China. One had only to visit the old China of the 1930's under Chiang Kai-shek to witness the realities of foreign domination—the special "International Settlements" in major ports under Western control, and subject to the laws of the Western powers; the Western "advisers" in government departments, in the armed forces and police;* the Western-owned factories and banks, and the Western-run newspapers and cinemas; and, above all, the Western gunboats lying menacingly in the river outside Shanghai, an ever-present reminder of the realities of power. Before long Japanese imperialism began to share more prominently in this domination of China, and in 1937 made her vain attempt to grab the entire booty for herself. After 1945, with the positions of her imperialist rivals greatly weakened, the United States attempted to step into Japan's shoes and turn China into her own neo-colonialist base. This bid by the United States also failed.

For the United States, the method of controlling a country without exercising direct political rule has been a long-standing one. For decades American imperialism pulled the strings in Liberia, determined its policies and ran its economy. The entire constitutional system was modelled on that of the United

---

* Former British members of the Shanghai police were to gain notoriety after 1948 in suppressing the liberation movement in Malaya.

States, and the Liberian currency was based on the dollar.

It was above all in Latin America, however, that the United States fashioned and practised this tactic. Outwardly Mexicans ruled Mexico, Venezuelans ruled Venezuela, the Bolivians ruled Bolivia, and so on. Porfirio Diaz, the hated dictator of Mexico, was a Mexican. Vincente Gomez, butcher of Venezuela, was a Venezuelan, as was the tyrant Jimenez who followed him. The bloody despot Trujillo was a son of San Domingo, and Batista, Cuba's sorrow, was Cuban-born. And it was the same in all twenty Latin American republics. Outwardly they were independent—and constitutionally speaking they were independent in fact. But real power was not in the hands of the people of these countries. It resided firmly in Wall Street and Washington, acting through a most fearsome and corrupt brood of dictators.

How U.S. domination of these territories was established has been described by one who helped to bring it about:

"I spent thirty-three years and four months in active service as a member of our country's most agile military force—the Marine Corps. I served in all commissioned ranks from second lieutenant to major-general. And during that period I spent most of my time being a high-class muscleman for Big Business, for Wall Street, and for the bankers. In short, I was a racketeer for capitalism . . .

"Thus, I helped to make Mexico and especially Tampico safe for American oil interests in 1914. I helped to make Haiti and Cuba a decent place for the National City Bank to collect revenues in . . . I helped purify Nicaragua for the international banking house of Brown Brothers in 1909–1912. I brought light to the Dominican Republic for American sugar interests in 1916. I helped make Honduras 'right' for American fruit companies in 1903 . . ."*

It was by a combination of financial control and political pressure (at all times resting on U.S. military might) that the

* Butler, Major General Smedley D.: *Common Sense*, November 1935.

United States was able to dominate Latin America. This domination also rested on the readiness of a small upper crust of indigenous corrupt politicians and grafters, together with semi-feudal landlords, to collaborate with the United States.

A striking case was that of Cuba before 1959.

> "The only foreign investments of importance (in Cuba) are those of the United States. American participation exceeds 90 per cent in the telephone and electric services, and about 50 per cent in public service railways, and roughly 40 per cent in raw sugar production. The Cuban branches of United States banks are entrusted with almost one fourth of all bank deposits . . ."*

Private American capital also owned most of the cattle ranches, and the major tourist facilities, and had a dominant position in oil. Even as early as 1933, it was estimated that United States interests held more than $1,500 million of property in Cuba.† A later estimate by the U.S. Department of Commerce put the figure of direct U.S. investments in Cuba in 1958 at $956 million.

Little attempt was made to hide the fact that successive U.S. Ambassadors in Cuba manipulated the local administration in the interests of American big business, and often for the direct benefit of the firms which the Ambassadors themselves represented. Arthur Gardner, U.S. Ambassador to Cuba from 1953 to 1957, was particularly concerned with the American-owned Cuban Telephone Company; he had no difficulty in securing an increase in its rates. His successor, Earl E. T. Smith, "received his appointment through the influence of John Hay Whitney, Republican National Campaign Treasurer."‡ Whitney was a large stockholder in Freeport Sulphur, one of whose subsidiaries was Moa Bay Mining Company. It is said that one of Smith's first official acts as Ambassador was to

---

* *Investment in Cuba*: U.S. Department of Commerce, 1956, p. 10.

† Scheer, Robert and Zeitlin, Maurice: *Cuba, An American Tragedy*, London, 1964, p. 48. See also New York, 1963 edition.

‡ ibid., p. 56.

secure a substantial tax reduction for the Moa Bay Mining Company.*

As in Cuba, so throughout Latin America. Such deception, robbery and domination was the reality of American relations with the countries to her south. American claims that she is not imperialist because she possesses no colonies are irrelevant to the real question. Quite apart from the fact that whenever it was convenient and possible the United States openly seized and held on to colonies as ruthlessly as any other imperialist power—as she did in Puerto Rico, Hawaii, the Virgin Islands, Alaska, various Pacific islands and, until 1946, the Philippines—and ignoring the fact that after World War II the United States annexed a number of Pacific Islands—the whole of Latin America was turned into a lucrative source of U.S. investment, limited in the main to producing raw materials, both agricultural and mineral, for American industry, commerce and consumption, and compelled to import most of her manufactured goods and machines from her northern neighbour.

America's "anti-colonialism" is a complete myth, for the real facts are that in Latin America the United States established one of the cruellest and most bloody empires the world has ever seen, and one moreover which has been immensely profitable for Wall Street. According to the United Nations Economic Commission for Latin America, the U.S. monopolies received, in the period 1946–56, 3·17 dollars for every dollar invested there; in the same period profits amounting to 5,600 million dollars were shipped back to the United States. In the fifteen years between 1947 and 1962 the influx of new U.S. investments in Latin America was 6,500 million dollars but the profits pumped out reached 10,000 million dollars. For a country "without colonies", the United States has done not at all badly.

The United States did not limit herself to taking profits. To make this possible, she directed and distorted the economies of the Latin American countries, condemned them to become

* ibid., p. 56.

largely dependent on one or two commodities each—such as coffee in Columbia, tin in Bolivia, copper in Chile, bananas in Honduras, oil and more recently iron ore in Venezuela—restricted their production of essential foodstuffs, and stifled their industrial growth. United States Ambassadors have acted as all-powerful monarchs, imposing their "advice" on nominally independent governments. This economic and political power has been backed up by military power, U.S. military advisers and instructors often playing a key role in the military services of the Latin American countries, which are tied to military aid programmes, agreements and alliances.

Thus, in essence, disguised methods of colonialism are not an entirely new form of colonial domination. Yet there is something new in the emergence of neo-colonialism. This is demonstrated by the fact that between 1945 and 1965 some 1,250,000 people in sixty countries liberated themselves from direct colonial rule and established their own sovereign governments. Before 1945 disguised forms of colonial domination were only practised in a minority of territories, mainly in Latin America, and only partially in the Middle East, Asia and Africa. Today, however, so headlong has been the retreat of direct colonial rule that it can be said that *neo-colonialism has now become the dominant form and is no longer the exception.*

The term, in fact, though it describes a *strategy* of imperialism and not a new *stage*, can only be understood as a strategy which has become predominant in a particular new phase of imperialism. This phase is one in which imperialism is faced with the emergence of a powerful socialist camp, an unprecedentedly powerful national liberation movement whose pulse can be felt now even in the smallest islands of Oceania, and a strong working class and democratic movement in the industrialised capitalist countries. The combination of these forces, and in particular the movement of the formerly oppressed peoples themselves which has become a flood of anti-colonial and anti-imperialist struggle, is sweeping away the old system of colonialism. It is the very disintegration of the system of direct colonial rule which has forced imperialism to turn to new tactics. The anti-colonial and anti-imperialist revolution has not been confined to any one continent, nor to the colonies of any single power. Imperialist power is being shaken to its very roots in Africa, Asia, the Middle East, Latin America and the Caribbean—and the imperialist states of the U.S., Britain, France, Portugal, Spain, Belgium, and Holland are being forced to surrender state power in their former possessions. It is clear that a most profound and powerful historical process is at work; this process is the end of direct colonial rule. The peoples of the world have weakened imperialism beyond repair. This epoch, which is witnessing the rise of socialism and the decline of capitalism, is also the epoch of the decline of colonialism.

Hence the turn by the imperialists to the strategy of neo-colonialism. This new policy is not a matter of choice but of desperate necessity. It is history which has driven the imperialists to adopt the mantle of neo-colonialism.

We have already noticed that indirect methods of domination have been tried out by the imperialists at an earlier stage. But the new phenomenon, neo-colonialism, is being attempted in the face of the emergence of a whole series of new states at a stage in world history in which these states are being drawn irresistibly towards socialism. The laws of socialism are increasingly determining the course of world history. Today all great popular movements, whether for peace, against fascism, against monopoly or for national independence, are being swept into the orbit of the great turnover of the world to socialism; and in this process they undergo changes and modifications in their initial character. Movements for national independence can no longer be confined within the limits of ordinary bourgeois democracy as in the nineteenth century, for these movements today are anti-imperialist movements taking place at a time of mounting socialist ascendancy in the world. The independent states in Asia, Africa and Latin America will increasingly turn in a socialist direction or make way for others that will certainly do so.

A major aim of neo-colonialism therefore, in addition to that of striving to continue the economic exploitation of the Third World, is to prevent the advance of the former colonial peoples to socialism. Hence the constant references by Western government spokesmen to the importance of keeping these countries "with the West". Hence the attempts to isolate them from the Soviet Union and other socialist states. And hence, too, the use of anti-communist propaganda to confuse the people.

In assessing what is new about neo-colonialism, it should be noted also that, on the basis of previous experience, imperialism has refined and elaborated its methods. New subtleties and agencies have been pressed into service, new instruments added, new personnel trained, new weapons used. Each imperialist power has its own particular contribution to make to the arsenal of neo-colonialist weapons and forms, but taken as a whole all these methods constitute a veritable system of neo-colonialism.

IMPERIALISM'S SEARCH FOR NEW ALLIES

That the Western powers were compelled to retreat in the face of the advancing national liberation movements after the second world war, and that they recognised the need to come to terms with reality and find a new basis for their activities is revealed in the statements of their leading spokesmen, who explain clearly both their dilemma and their new tactics. Thus, at the beginning of 1960, "Africa Year", in which a whole series of African states won their independence, Harold Macmillan, at that time British Premier, made his famous "wind of change" speech in Cape Town.* In the course of his remarks he said:

"The most striking of all the impressions I have formed since I left London a month ago, is of the strength of this African national consciousness . . . The wind of change is blowing through the continent.

"Whether we like it or not, this growth of national con-

* Macmillan, Harold: Speech to the House of Assembly, Cape Town, South Africa, February 3, 1960.

sciousness is a political fact. We must all accept it as a fact. Our national policies must take account of it . . . I sincerely believe that if we cannot do so, we may imperil the precarious balance of East and West . . . As I see it, the great issue in this second half of the twentieth century is whether the uncommitted peoples of Asia and Africa will swing to the East or to the West. Will they be drawn into the Communist camp?"

The same recognition of the realities of the situation and of the need to work out a new approach is to be found in the speech made by General de Gaulle to French officers at Blida, on December 9, 1960, a full year before the cease-fire agreement was made with the Algerian F.L.N. In this speech De Gaulle pleaded with his army officers to appreciate what was happening in the world, to understand that the old methods of outright suppression and domination by force of arms and the direct exercise of state power were becoming impossible, and that a new way must be found for "the work of France in Algeria" to "go on". As the speech makes clear, it was not for De Gaulle a matter of choice (and he makes no attempt to hide his regret at what is taking place) but a question of facing the facts of life.

"The work of France in Algeria must go on, and it is only too evident that it cannot go on under the conditions of yesterday. One may regret this, and you will realise that a man of my age and background may have his regrets at that which probably could have been done earlier and which was left undone. . . .

"But when one assumes national responsibilities one must take the problem as a whole, as it is—and such as it is, it cannot be dealt with as in days gone by . . .

". . . the insurrection, and all that is connected with it, is taking place in a new world, in a world which is not at all like the world I knew myself when I was young. There is— you are well aware of this—the whole context of emancipation which is sweeping the world from one end to another, which has swept over our Black Africa, which has swept, without exception, over all those which once were empires, and which cannot but have considerable consequences here . . .''

In these two speeches one can sense the historic dilemma of the Western powers. Neither De Gaulle nor Macmillan greets the growth of national consciousness, the sweep of "the insurrection", with open arms. On the contrary, their words are full of forebodings and sentiments of regret. Yet they also make clear that there is no intention of complete retreat; only of finding a new basis on which to operate.

For the United States the dilemma was equally acute—and the policy elaborated to meet the new situation basically the same. For all the imperialist powers, the changed circumstances in which they found themselves meant an obligation to find new positions from which they could work not merely to maintain the essence of their former influence and safeguard their interests but to launch new attacks against the national liberation movements, and above all, to ensure that "the uncommitted peoples of Asia and Africa . . . swing . . . to the West".

In the immediate post-1945 situation, as previously pointed out, the Western powers had striven to crush the movements for national liberation—in Indo-china, Indonesia, Malaya, India, Korea, the Philippines, Madagascar and throughout Africa. By 1960 this had become impossible, except in a few special cases. First in Asia, and then in Africa, the movements for independence had become so powerful, and the world relation of forces meanwhile so altered, that the Western powers had to recognise the facts of life and allow the establishment of new independent states. In this situation, they decided to bend with the wind, to go along with the national movements with the intention of obtaining a foothold within them, of exerting pressure on them, and moulding them to suit Western interests. Thus, Mr. Chester Bowles, former U.S. Ambassador to India, recommended the United States to "identify our own self-interests with theirs", that is to say, with the national liberation movements; and further, to "identify itself boldly with the social, economic and political revolution."*

Similarly, Sir Andrew Cohen, former head of the Africa Department of the Colonial Office, a former Governor of Uganda, and subsequently head of the Department of Technical Co-operation which has since been merged with the Ministry for Overseas Development, has argued that "successful co-operation with nationalism is our greatest bulwark against communism in Africa."† Explaining that "nationalist movements are bound to grow steadily more powerful", he suggested that "The intelligent thing is for Governments to recognise this early, and by skilful anticipation to try and guide the energies of nationalists into constructive channels".‡ In this way, he hoped, the national movements would remain "friendly to the Western world".¶

To carry through this tactic, the Western powers realised that they would have to find allies within the new states who would co-operate with the West, and allow their countries to remain within the orbit of Western influence—economically, politically, militarily and ideologically. Such co-operation could seldom be absolute and all-embracing, except in the case of a few utterly unrepresentative puppets such as Syngman Rhee followed by Pak Jung Hi in Korea, or Diem followed by Ky in South Vietnam.

Elsewhere, it was rather a question of seeking out social and political forces which, in their own class interests, would not push the national revolution too far nor allow the actions of their people to endanger too greatly the interests of the Western powers. In most cases, the old pre-capitalist strata—feudal landlords, princes, rajahs, sheiks and chiefs—were too discredited. They had been a bulwark of the old colonial systems,

* Bowles, Chester: *The Conscience of a Liberal,* New York, 1962.

† Cohen, Sir Andrew: *British Policy in Changing Africa,* London, 1959, p. 61.

‡ ibid.   ¶ ibid., p. 114.

and were no longer trusted by the people. The very fact that they had been protected and propped up by imperialist troops rendered them of little immediate value to imperialism in the new stage. These old traditional rulers had been such obvious enemies of the national liberation movements that the winning of national independence constituted a blow against them as well as against colonialism.

Moreover, whereas the traditional rulers had been content to maintain the same economic and social system that had existed for decades, the new rulers thrown up by the national movements represented classes which were interested in creating modern states, new industries, universities, towns and parliamentary institutions. This could not be done on the basis of feudalism, still less of tribalism.

The Western powers have understood that in this new epoch they can only have influence in the new states by operating via the new social forces which have been thrown up into positions of power by the national revolutions; and this means, above all, the new élite—the petty-bourgeoisie, the intelligentsia, the new administrators, technicians and military leaders, and the emerging indigenous capitalist forces.

If, as we have seen, the old system of colonial rule was, in essence, an alliance between external imperialism and local pre-capitalist forces, then neo-colonialism generally represents a new alliance, one between external imperialism and sections of the local bourgeoisie and petty-bourgeoisie. Of course, in most cases, the alliance is more complex. Even before independence, sections of the local capitalist class, as in Asia, were ready to co-operate with imperialism, although primarily the alliance under colonialism was with pre-capitalist forces. With the emergence of new states, the imperialists still utilise their old connections with feudalism and with tribal chiefs, as the experience of Nigeria, Ghana, Niger, Malaya, Indonesia and the Sudan indicate only too well. In some cases, such elements, in alliance with new capitalist forces, have constituted the new governments. In other cases, where they have been squeezed out of positions of power, they have been held in reserve by imperialism, as a form of pressure against the new states, or thrown into battle whenever the moment seems opportune or the need is urgently present, in order to create difficulties, promote division and tension and so hinder the advance of these states.

Under colonialism, for economic as well as political reasons, the imperialist powers were mainly concerned to maintain the feudal or semi-feudal structure of the colonies, treating these territories solely as agrarian hinterlands for their own industrialised economies. Today, acting under conditions of neo-colonialism, they can no longer limit their aims entirely in this way. In a world which is turning towards socialism, the Western powers are concerned above all to keep the former colonies from breaking out of the orbit of capitalism. However heavy hang the burdens of feudalism and tribalism on these new states, no one seriously advocates the maintenance of such patterns of society as being suitable for the kind of transformations needed in the twentieth century. The growth of new class forces in the Third World, and the pressure within the new states to build modern viable economies and political systems faces the peoples with only two choices: either to take the capitalist path, or to strike out along the non-capitalist path in the direction of socialism. An essential aim of neo-colonialism, therefore, is to keep the new states from marching in the direction of socialism. Unable to preserve feudal or semi-feudal societies as the mainstay of their influence, the imperialists are striving to push the new states along a capitalist path, and openly to encourage and foster new capitalist forces which they hope will assist this task, without making it possible for such forces to become strong enough to end their dependence on imperialism. This, too, is an essential feature of neo-colonialism.

In many parts of Africa, where colonialism and white settler domination made the emergence of a capitalist class very difficult, the deliberate nurturing of such a class, commonly referred to as "a middle class", has been openly proclaimed by Western leaders as essential to this new phase. The Joint East African and Central Board placed its hopes on the prospect that "an African middle class will emerge."* Similarly, the Federal Republic of Germany, in the general principles it laid down for its conference of West German diplomatists at Addis Ababa, October 1959, did not forget to emphasise that its policy towards Africa should be based on the understanding that "the social and economic structure must be stabilised by the building up of a middle class" in the different African territories.† These suggestions have in practice been followed both by Western Governments and by major monopoly firms operating in such territories.‡

The same motive to create a new capitalist ally lay behind all the Western-sponsored schemes for land reform in Asia and Africa after 1945. Under such schemes, while feudalism and communal land systems were weakened, the majority of peasants remained without land (or with insufficient good land), were denied credits, and were too poor to buy machines, good quality seeds, chemical fertilisers and pesticides. At the same time a stratum of richer peasants came into existence, employing wage labour, and former landlords often became large-scale capitalist farmers.¶ It was on this stratum that the Western powers placed their hopes of providing a barrier to revolutionary change in the countryside.

Neo-colonialism, as can be seen from the foregoing, is essentially a product of the new epoch in which we live. It is a temporary tactic of declining imperialism, but a dying animal can be vicious and dangerous. Neo-colonialism has already caused heavy damage to the national liberation movements, and will yet do more harm before it is finally laid to rest.

Its aims have been outlined—to preserve imperialist economic and strategic interests. This requires not only that former colonial countries remain under imperialist domination in

* *East Africa and Rhodesia*, 23 April, 1959, p. 991.

† *The Times*, November 17, 1959.

‡ For more details see Woddis, Jack: *Africa—The Lion Awakes*, London, 1961, pp. 162–196.

¶ See: Woddis, Jack: "Asia's Peasants in Revolt" (*Modern Quarterly*, Vol. 8, No. 2. 1953); and Woddis, Jack: *Africa, the Roots of Revolt*, London, 1960, p. 31 et. foll.

other forms so as to provide maximum profits for it, but that, alongside this process of robbery, a degree of indigenous capitalism should develop within these countries. There are two reasons for this latter aim of nourishing capitalism in the new states, one mainly economic, the other mainly political. The economic motive behind the calculation to build capitalism is that the feudal and other pre-capitalist forms of economy in the Third World have become barriers to their very exploitation by the big foreign monopolies. These countries have been so robbed and so held back that their ability to provide adequate profits for all the imperialist powers who wish to expand their export of capital and expand their trade (and to provide for a new local ruling class as well as coping with the expectations of the people) requires a measure of economic change which will lead to an expansion of the market, and, to a limited extent, to technological development. Such economic change means a partial break with pre-capitalist forms of economy.

The political motive arises from the world competition between the two systems of capitalism and socialism. The imperialist powers naturally wish as much of the world as possible to remain capitalist. They see their world being eroded, country after country falling into the hands of its own workers and peasants. All their imperialist political calculations, all their military plans—which require literally hundreds of overseas bases—will be upset if they are unable to continue their dominion over most of the world. Furthermore, the advance of socialism lowers their prestige and starts to undermine their very morale. The ideas of socialism and communism attract increasing millions of people from decade to decade. The great fear of the imperialists is that the majority of their own working people in the metropolitan bases will begin to question capitalism, will begin to think that if the rest of the world is turning to socialism there must be something in it. Hence, imperialism, through the agency of neo-colonialism, is striving to nourish capitalism in the new states, to foster a class with which it can co-operate, to give a fresh injection into the world system of capitalism, and to halt the drift to socialism which they feel is steadily drawing away the ground beneath them as the outgoing tide sucks away the sand from under one's feet by the edge of the sea.

In endeavouring to operate neo-colonialism, the imperialists have devised a whole series of forms which they regard as essential to the fulfilment of their plans—forms which are conditioned by and grow out of the very aims of neo-colonialism. It is therefore essential to understand more precisely what neo-colonialism is and how it actually operates.

3

Neo-Colonialism at Work

The problem of neo-colonialism is sometimes presented as if it were solely a question of imperialism retaining and extending its economic control and influence after it has been compelled to surrender its political state power. Of course, economic aims are a decisive element of neo-colonialism, but it would be wrong to limit the concept in this way. All those who have had direct experience of neo-colonialism describe it as a far more complex and more comprehensive phenomenon. The Third All-African People's Conference, meeting in Cairo in March 1961, assessing the new dangers arising for the independent states in Africa, adopted a special resolution on neo-colonialism, together with another resolution on "The Liquidation of the Remnants of Imperialism". These two resolutions describe, in considerable detail, the forms and methods of neo-colonialism and help one to understand its all-embracing character. They stress that "neo-colonialism, which is the survival of the colonial system in spite of formal recognition of political independence in emerging countries which become the victims of an indirect and subtle form of domination by *political, economic, social, military or technical means*, is the greatest threat to African countries that have newly won their independence or those approaching this status."

Kwame Nkrumah, too, has explained that the methods of the neo-colonialists are "subtle and varied" and that the neo-colonialists "operate not only in the economic field, but also in the political, religious, ideological and cultural spheres."*

* Nkrumah, Kwame: *Neo-Colonialism, The Last Stage of Imperialism*, London, 1965, p. 239. See also New York edition.

In the same way, the resolution on "Colonialism and Neo-colonialism" adopted at the First Afro-Asian-Latin American People's Solidarity Conference, held in Havana, January 3–12, 1966, emphasises the all-round character of neo-colonialism:

> "To guarantee its domination, imperialism tries to destroy the national, cultural and spiritual values of each country, and forms an apparatus of domination which includes national armed forces docile to their policy, the establishment of military bases, the creation of organs of repression, with technical advisers from imperialist countries, the signing of secret military pacts, the formation of regional and international warmongering alliances. It encourages and carries out coups d'état and political assassinations to ensure puppet governments; at the same time, in the economic field it resorts to deceptive formulas, such as the so-called Alliance for Progress, Food for Peace and other similar forms, while using international institutions such as the International Monetary Fund and the International Bank for Reconstruction and Development to reinforce its economic domination."

MOVING TO PREPARED POSITIONS

A full description of all the methods used by neo-colonialism could fill volumes; but an examination of some of its forms is essential for our understanding of neo-colonialism. Two general observations need to be made first, however. The resolution of the Third All-African People's Conference rightly draws attention to the fact that neo-colonialism commences its operations even before the achievement of national independence. In other words, neo-colonialism is a deliberate move to prepared positions. It has already been noted that in the period immediately following the second world war, the Western powers, faced with the necessity of retreating in the face of the advancing national movements in Asia, did everything possible to prevent Communists and other consistent anti-imperialists from participating in the new governments then emerging.

Wherever they sensed that they would have to give way and concede political independence the Western powers strove to ensure that state power did not fall into the hands of those who were not prepared to co-operate with imperialism.

They eagerly sought out and supported the most conservative and right-wing forces in the Third World *and strove to bring them out on top before conceding independence*. This policy, which was pursued in Asia after 1945, was to be tried out later both in Africa and in the Caribbean, as the most recent examples indicate.

In Basutoland (now Lesotho), as the pressure for independence grew, steps were taken to bring the most politically conservative forces out on top. Elections in April 1965, prior to independence, gave a majority of votes to the Basutoland Congress Party and the Marematlou Freedom Party; but the British Government, despite protests, handed over power to Chief Leabua, and his "National Party", which was openly backed by the Republic of South Africa and by West Germany.* Swaziland does not yet enjoy independence, but here, too, in anticipation of such an achievement, the British Government has again taken steps to ensure that the most conservative political forces in the country are the ones to whom power will be given. Constitutional proposals published in March 1966 propose independence for Swaziland in 1970. The proposals provide for Swaziland to be an independent kingdom, under King Sobhuza II, with special guarantees for the 2,000 strong white minority which itself backs the royalist Imbokodvo Party. Neither the Swaziland Progressive Party nor the Ngwane Liberatory Congress were represented at the conference which prepared the new constitution; and both these parties have called for its rejection. But the British Government, true to its neo-colonialist ambitions, is determined to assist the conservative and traditional forces to

* Since independence, Chief Leabua has taken drastic steps to crush the opposition.

become the Government of Swaziland when it becomes independent in 1970.

In Guyana, throughout the period from 1953, when the People's Progressive Party, led by Dr. Cheddi Jagan, first won the elections and formed the Government under the then-existing system of limited internal self-government, the British and United States Governments have done everything possible to make sure that a P.P.P. Government was not in power at the time of granting independence. Dr. Jagan and his Ministers were first removed in 1953, after 133 days in office; an Emergency was declared, the Constitution suspended, and Dr. Jagan and other leaders imprisoned. After a lapse of four years elections were allowed again, in 1957—but not before divisions had been created in the P.P.P., at first on an anti-Communist basis, but subsequently through the incitement of racialist prejudice. Despite these difficulties, the P.P.P. emerged as victors once again. But the Government still refused to grant independence. In the 1961 elections, the P.P.P. won for the third time running, this time gaining twenty seats out of the thirty-five. Once again, the British Government refused to grant Guyana independence. Increasingly it was made clear in the British and American press that, quite apart from the British Government's own wishes, the United States was determined not to have Dr. Jagan and the P.P.P. heading an independent Government in Guyana. "One Cuba was enough", was their excuse. After fires and widespread arson in 1962, resulting in some $40 million damage, and of C.I.A. engineered strikes and riots in 1963,* in which violent attacks

* See Jagan, Cheddi: *The West on Trial*, London, 1966, p. 303 et foll. The charges first made by Dr. Jagan have been largely confirmed by the revelations which followed the March 1967 issue of the American journal, *Ramparts*. It appears that CIA funds were channelled via an organisation known as the Gotham Foundation, which in turn passed on the funds to Dr. Jagan's opponents in Guyana via the Public Services International, a trade secretariat of the International Confederation of Free Trade Unions, dominated by the American unions affiliated to this body. In February 1967, Dr. Arnold Zander, head of the principal American union affiliated to the PSI, confessed that his own union had received considerable sums of

were made on Government buildings and on Ministers—the British Government found that it had still not forced the overthrow of the P.P.P. Government. It thereupon introduced new constitutional changes at the end of 1963, providing for fresh elections, before the expiry of the term of office of the P.P.P. Government, and based on a system of proportional representation which could only intensify racial voting. It was open press comment in Britain at the time that the decision of the British Government not to grant independence to the P.P.P. Government was motivated largely by a desire to placate the United States. *The Scotsman* commented that "It is certainly true that the Americans have made no secret of their antipathy to Dr. Jagan and his Marxist views . . . their views must certainly have been in Mr. Sandys' mind when he made his decision."* Writing in *The Guardian*, Mr. H. Hassal pinpointed what he regarded as the main motives behind the manoeuvres to refuse conceding independence to Guyana at that time:

". . . the hatred of Jagan, the fear of any brand of Socialism and the safeguarding of the Hemisphere economically for Standard Oil, International Telephone, the United Fruit Company and others . . ."†

Terrorist actions against the P.P.P. and its supporters continued throughout 1964—and neither the police, nor the British armed forces then present, nor the Governor would take the necessary steps to stop them. The intention of the British and U.S. rulers to make life impossible for the P.P.P. Government was obvious. It was under these difficult conditions that elections in Guyana were held in December 1964, the newly elected Labour Government in Britain refusing to

money from the CIA between 1958 and 1964. Two American citizens who were seen constantly in Guyana during the 1963 "strike"—Mr. William Doherty and Mr. Howard McCabe—are both PSI officials. (See *The Guardian*, April 17, 1967.)

* Quoted in Jagan, Cheddi: op. cit., p. 322.
† ibid.

set aside the anti-democratic constitutional changes introduced by its Tory predecessor. Again the P.P.P. emerged as the strongest party. It secured 45·8 per cent of the votes, an increase of 3·2 per cent over 1961; the People's National Congress (P.N.C.), led by Forbes Burnham, secured 40·5 per cent, a decrease of 0·4 per cent; and the United Force, 12·4 per cent, a decrease of 3·9 per cent. The P.P.P. alleged considerable irregularities to have taken place during the elections. There was certainly something strange about the proxy vote of 7,000; the P.P.P. received only 8·6 per cent of these, compared with its 45·8 per cent of the total votes.

Without giving Dr. Jagan the chance to form a Government, the Governor called on Mr. Burnham, who formed a coalition with the United Force. With the P.P.P. forced out of office, the British Government, apparently reassured by a nod from Wall Street and Washington, was happy to "grant independence" to Guyana.

The consequences were not long in following. U.S. loans, U.S. advisers, the "Peace Corps", U.S. military and police instructors, U.S. training schemes, the transference to a U.S. company of the handling of Guyana's rice trade, U.S. help to extend the airfield, a deal with the powerful U.S. Reynolds Metal Company, and the granting of concessions to big American and British oil companies. As Dr. Jagan has rightly commented, independent Guyana is being "put up for auction"—and the main bidder is the United States.

The bitter experience of Guyana fully bears out the point stressed in the resolution of the All-African People's Conference that neo-colonialism is a great threat to countries "approaching" independence.

The manoeuvre carried out in Guyana, Lesotho and Swaziland was practised earlier in Malaya and Malta. It was also tried in Zanzibar, but within 33 days of the island gaining independence at the end of 1963, the government favoured by Britain was overthrown by an armed rising supported by the people.

The resolution adopted by the Third All-African People's Conference significantly added Israel and South Africa to the list of countries practising neo-colonialism. In the case of Israel, one can note her military actions in the Middle East, as well as her activities in Africa, in connection with which she has set up, with the aid of U.S. funds, a special trade union college in Israel. The Republic of South Africa is playing a particular rôle in helping to maintain European domination over a wide area of southern and central Africa, as shown by its activities in relation to South West Africa, the former High Commission Territories, Malawi, Southern Rhodesia, and the Portuguese colonies.

One other general point needs to be made before examining in more detail the different methods and forms of neo-colonialism. The main countries practising neo-colonialism are Britain, France, the United States and Western Germany. It will be noticed that the first two of these four countries had substantial colonial empires at the end of the second world war, while the latter two, although imperialist powers, were without colonial possessions.* In practising neo-colonialism, countries such as Britain and France suffer certain disadvantages as compared with the United States or West Germany. Britain and France are known as former colonial powers and have been a main target of the national liberation movements, by whom they are naturally regarded with considerable suspicion after independence. The United States, on the other hand, comes in the guise of an "anti-colonial" power, without the burden of a vast colonial empire to explain away. Further, Britain and France have been considerably weakened economically since the war, while the United States is the dominant force in the capitalist world and its major military power. (These arguments about the United States apply largely to West Germany as well.)

Britain and France, however, start off with considerable cards in their hands as well, even though they are economically and militarily less powerful. They already have all the neces-

---

* The United States, as noticed earlier, had *some* colonial possessions, but its main sphere of domination and investment was in Latin America where it did not exercise direct state power.

sary connections and know-how; they have for years been on the spot, able to sound out people, to win over supporters from the new élite as well as from the traditional rulers, to encourage British or French patterns of thought, to train military and technical cadres in their own institutions, to make use of personnel from the metropolis who have specialised for decades in the problems of the new states, know the countries, their languages, and their people, are familiar with their problems and so on. They are therefore able at first to ensure that their nationals are retained in the new states, in key state and economic positions, as well as in educational and ideological institutions. Moreover, their previous political rule has made it possible for them to own and control the key sectors of the economy of the new states. A country emerging from colonialism is virtually the economic plaything of the monopolies connected directly with the former colonial power.

For all these reasons, a country like the United States cannot practise neo-colonialism in Africa and most of Asia in the same way as can the former colonial powers. It virtually has to *break its way in*. Hence the ready use of military force by the United States to establish its neo-colonialist base against both the former colonial power as well as against the indigenous national independence movements themselves, as for example in South Vietnam and Congo (Kinshasa). Hence the fantastic and open spending of millions of dollars simply to buy over individuals who would otherwise feel a certain allegiance and pull towards the former ruling country. Hence the despatch of thousands of "Peace Corps" workers to provide a heavy force of Americans "on the ground" in competition with the thousands of British, French, or Belgian nationals who have already been there for years. And hence, too, the heavy reliance on the C.I.A. to gain rapidly by open assassination and coups d'état the key political positions and economic high-points which the older colonial powers had achieved through years of patient work and with all the advantages of being the power in possession.

Neo-colonialism, therefore, takes place under conditions of acute competition and rivalry between the major imperialist powers, and this very conflict gives rise to divisions and instability in many of the new states which assist the aims of the neo-colonialists. The seven year old conflict in Congo (Kinshasa), for example, is not simply one between the national liberation movement and imperialism; it is equally conditioned and shaped by the fierce conflict between the various imperialist powers themselves, the United States striving to weaken or oust the former Anglo-Belgian alliance, and France and West Germany attempting to gain their footholds, too. Even Italy and Japan are now entering the scene.

Despite their conflicts with one another, however, the imperialists are finding it increasingly necessary to combine their forces in order to hold back the national independence movements. Collective forms of neo-colonialism, economic and military, are being forged, as a means of safeguarding and intensifying the exploitation of the Third World. At the same time, each imperialist power strives to group around itself and under its domination a number of new states which it hopes will thus remain, in effect, its dependencies.

The South East Asia Treaty Organisation (SEATO) and the Central Asia Treaty Organisation (CENTO) have now been supplemented by the U.S.-sponsored Asian and Pacific military alliance known as ASPAC. The United States is working for a similar military alliance in Latin America, either through widening the scope of the existing Inter-American Defence Board or by setting up a new Inter-American Force (IAF). In the Middle East there have been the moves to establish an Islamic Pact, based on the most conservative and pro-Western states in the area, and directed against the most consistently anti-imperialist states, especially the United Arab Republic. In the economic sphere, the United States has established the Alliance for Progress covering Latin America; Britain has tried to utilise the Colombo Plan in Asia; and France and West Germany have utilised the European Common Market to intensify their exploitation of the "associated states" in Africa. For Britain, the Commonwealth has been particularly useful, both as an idea to which some heads of new states have felt themselves drawn, and as an institution through which links with British imperialism are maintained. Japan, too, has sought to establish a new grouping in the Far East, based on her growing influence and investments in Taiwan and South Korea, but with economic and political ambitions reaching much further afield, and recalling her earlier plans for a "Co-prosperity sphere".

The main driving force behind these economic and military alliances is the United States, which has become the principal supporter of neo-colonialism throughout the world. Without the economic and military backing of the United States, the whole structure of neo-colonialism would collapse to the ground. At the same time, within this imperialist alliance itself, the United States moves all the time against the positions of its weaker allies, striving to become the inheritor of their former empires though without ruling these territories directly as colonial possessions. Thus, in the past twenty years, the United States has replaced Japan in South Korea, ousted the French in South Vietnam, ended British and Japanese influence in Thailand, and is pressing on British and French toes throughout Africa, Asia, the Middle East and the Caribbean.

NEO-COLONIALISM'S POLITICAL WEAPONS

There are four main fields in which neo-colonialist activities are expressed—political, ideological, military and economic. It is not possible in this short booklet to examine these in any detail, but it is useful to draw attention to some of the main ways in which neo-colonialism operates.

In the political field, one can note at the outset British imperialist insistence on participating in drawing up the constitution of countries about to become independent. In this way, in addition to suggesting clauses which will directly safeguard its interests, it makes proposals intended to saddle the new states with problems which weaken them and enable the old game of "divide and rule" to be continued even after independence. Sometimes this takes the form of complete partition, as in the case of India and Pakistan (with the added problem of Kashmir thrown in for good measure). Sometimes, as in the case of Nigeria, regionalism within the territory is the means utilised. Attempts were made to impose similar regionalist patterns on Ghana and Kenya, but these failed in the face of the refusal of the national movements to accept such a structure. France played the same game of divide and rule in Africa; the two administrative blocs—French Equatorial Africa and French West Africa—were split up into fourteen different states, each with only a few million inhabitants. French influence was able subsequently to link most of these together with Malagasy into the Common Organisation of African States and Malagasy (OCAM).* The existence of so many separate states within this grouping has made it easier for France to continue its influence over each as well as over the whole in a way which might not have been so easy if larger independent states had been created out of the former French colonies in Africa. In Latin America, the United States has fully utilised the Organisation of American States (OAS) as an institution through which it can exercise its power over the whole continent, acting behind the mask of a regional organisation of independent states instead of having to act always in its own direct name.

A major political objective of all the imperialist powers is to influence the key personnel in the new states. In the case of former colonial powers, it is possible, at least in the first years of independence, to ensure that former colonial officials and civil servants from the metropolis are retained in different posts in the state, including economic institutions, the police and the armed forces. Their whole background, training and outlook ill fits them for assisting the newly liberated peoples, and they become an obstacle to genuine advance. In Malaysia and Singapore, as well as in Malawi and Kenya, British intelligence officers are still employed by the independent governments of these countries. Numerous Belgian "advisers" are to be found in government and state positions in Congo (Kinshasa), as are French "advisers" in most of the former French

* Guinea and Mali do not belong to OCAM.

colonies in Africa. There may be some former colonial officials who sincerely wish to assist the new states, but the majority of them, whatever may be their views, are willy-nilly part of the imperialist establishment which trained them, moulded their outlook and continues to retain them precisely because they are still able to render a service.

In addition to the retention of former colonial officials and civil servants, the colonial powers have taken steps to train and send out to the new states additional personnel who are employed as technicians, advisers and consultants. The British Government has even set up a special Department of Technical Co-operation, under Sir Andrew Cohen, former head of the African Department of the Colonial Office. This new Department was started off with a staff of one thousand and a financial allocation of £30 million. *The Times* commented (26 June 1962) that visitors from the new States to the Department "do not feel that it bears the taint of neo-colonialism". It may not officially bear the "taint", but neo-colonialism is its real purpose, and since it was established it has been busily engaged in training, selecting and placing British personnel (some of whom have previously worked in British colonies) in positions in the new states. In liaison with British intelligence services, this Department also ensures a close scrutiny of all individuals who apply for overseas posts via its channels, and sees to it that those who are regarded as politically unsuitable are rejected. Since the advent of a Labour Government, this Department has been taken over by the new Ministry of Overseas Development, but that astute initiator of much of Britain's neo-colonialist policy, Sir Andrew Cohen, is still retained and is generally regarded as the power behind the Ministry, whoever happens to hold the official post of Minister at any particular time.

The changing shape of the British Commonwealth is finding other appropriate changes in the structure of the British Government's institutions. The Colonial Office has now been wound up, and becomes the Dependent Territories Division of the Commonwealth Office—itself the new name for the merged Commonwealth Relations Office and Colonial Office. At the same time, it should not be thought that this means an actual diminution of the activity of British imperialist institutions in relation to the colonies and former colonies. In fact, as the *Times* reminds us (30 July 1966): "The Colonial Office has for many years been expanding its specialist and technical services. Many of these specialists are now to be found in the Ministry of Overseas Development. Others continue by invitation to work for governments which they have earlier helped to independence, which is all in the tradition."

For former colony-owning states such as France and Britain the placing of personnel in the new states is, in many ways, more simple than it is for the United States or West Germany, at least in the initial stages. The latter do not straight away have the necessary contacts; sometimes even language presents a problem. For this reason they are obliged to use different methods and even create new institutions in order to secure the placing of their own personnel in the new states.

One such institution is the American "Peace Corps", which has now been in existence for five years. Official propaganda in the United States, and to some extent in Britain, has attempted to present the Corps as a body of idealistic young Americans who, in a noble spirit of dedication and self-sacrifice, have given up their comfortable conditions at home to work in uncongenial climates and under primitive conditions in order to assist the developing countries to build up their economies and their social and cultural institutions. There may well be such sincere individuals among the members of the Peace Corps, but ironically the very presence and behaviour of such personnel helps to mask its true character and even to assist its real purposes. Directed by Robert Sargent Shriver, a former manager of a large U.S. trading firm, and a one-time member of the Office of Strategic Services (O.S.S.), and of the Central Intelligence Agency (C.I.A.), the Corps comes under the "foreign assistance" programmes of the U.S. State Department, and acts on the basis of the "mutual security law", its expenses being listed in the Federal Budget under "mutual security".

Already by 1963 its annual budget was over $100 million.

The Peace Corps, even if its members are not all aware of it, assists the C.I.A. by providing it with additional sources of information, especially on individuals and economic developments. The most innocent-seeming snapshots of beauty spots, of new buildings, of interesting terrain—all are invaluable raw material for the C.I.A.* A further role of the Peace Corps is to popularise "the American way of life", and it is precisely in this field that a few well-meaning innocents unwittingly assist. The ideological role of the Corps is indicated by the very high proportion of its members who are employed as teachers. It has been reported that at least half the faculty in every Ethiopian secondary school is a Peace Corps member. In Sierra Leone, a quarter of the teachers are American. In Tanzania, it was stated by President Nyerere in 1965 that, by a strange coincidence, opposition to his proposals on the one party system and the constitutional changes then being proposed came primarily from students attending schools where the teachers were American Peace Corps members.

The importance attached to the Peace Corps by the American Government is shown by its rapid growth—from 700 "volunteers" working in 13 countries in 1961, to 5,000 members in 45 countries in 1963, with a 1965 target of 14,500 overseas workers. After a visit to Washington in 1963, Mr. Philip Goodhart, British Member of Parliament, reported that recruitment to the Corps was taking place at the rate of 3,000 a month. Of the 3,000, after a check-up comparable with "the vetting procedure of our own (i.e. British) security services", about one in five are selected.† People with left-wing or progressive views are rigidly excluded by the U.S. security forces.

The example of the U.S. Peace Corps has been followed by West Germany which has established similar bodies with the

* The recent revelations concerning the C.I.A.'s., secret connections with the American National Student Association throw further light on the methods of this organisation. (See *The Times*, February 15, 1967, and the March 1967 issue of *Ramparts*.)

† *Daily Telegraph*, September 12, 1963.

same objective in mind. In 1963 the West German government set up a German Development Service, an organisation of "development aiders" based on the American Peace Corps model. At its founding ceremony, the Development Aid Minister described the new Service as "a new and perhaps the most important instrument of our development policy."* There is little attempt to hide the real purposes of the Service. "The new corps is in the first place political; this is unarmed guerrilla warfare."† Significantly, the director of the U.S. Peace Corps himself, Robert Sargent Shriver, visited West Germany in 1964 to advise the West German Government on its Development Service, which the West German press admits is based on the American model. The first "development aiders"—35 of them—started work in mid-1964. The extension of this service was expected to take place very rapidly, the 1965 aim being 1,000 members already working overseas. The annual expenditure on the project is ten million marks.

This is by no means the full extent of special West German agencies to penetrate the developing countries in the interests of the West German monopolies and state interests. There is, for example, the Institute for International Solidarity, which is financed both by the Christian Democrat Party and by the State. One report states that the annual subsidy for this institute from the federal budget is 4·5 million marks.‡ One of the functions of this Institute and its leading personnel is to intervene politically and financially in the affairs of other countries. Its particular target is Latin America. The Institute was founded in 1962 by Heinrich Gewandt, a Christian Democrat member of Parliament. Its directors include the West German Defence Minister, Kai Uwe von Hassel, and two other Ministers, Heck and Dollinger. The aims of this institute as described in the West German press are "to influence the

* *Bulletin des Presse und Informationsamtes der Bundesregierung*, Bonn, June 25, 1963.

† *Kolnische Rundschau*, May 19, 1963.

‡ *Der Spiegel*, Hamburg, 12, 1965.

economic and social structure of these countries (i.e. especially Latin America) by establishing contacts with young politicians and economists."*

In concentrating on Latin America, this West German Institute has attracted the sympathetic interest of the U.S. State Department which does not always find it convenient to pursue its objectives in Latin America too openly. In 1963, Gewandt visited the U.S. State Department. According to *Der Spiegel*,† he was given every encouragement with his plans since "Washington was looking for allies in Latin America in its struggle against rapidly growing Fidelism." A specific task of the Institute is the founding of Christian Democratic Parties in Latin America. In this respect, it is common knowledge in West Germany as well as in Chile, that Gewandt and his Institute played a prominent part in securing the electoral victory of Eduard Frei and his Christian Democrat Party in the 1964 elections in Chile.

> "Although Eduard Frei, candidate of the Christian Democrats, won the absolute majority, the candidate of the Popular Front, Salvador Allende, won 46 per cent of all the votes. What would have been the result of the elections if the Christian Democrats of the Federal Republic had not energetically intervened in favour of Frei, using various means, including money?"‡

West Germany did not have to wait long before making use of its new ally. A special "assistance" programme was drawn up in Bonn for the new government in Chile. "Chilean politicians and journalists", wrote *Der Spiegel*¶ "soon noticed that the planned reforms of the new Frei government sometimes resembled Federal German laws to the very wording."

Another function of Gewandt's Institute is that of training

---

* *Der Kurier*, West Berlin, January 13, 1965.

† 12, 1965.

‡ *Handelsblatt*, Dusseldorf, October 16–17, 1964. See also, *Der Spiegel*, 12, 1965: "Heinrich Gewandt can boast of helping decisively to achieve victory for Eduardo Frei".   ¶ ibid.

personnel from the developing countries, in order to be able to influence potential leaders. A report in *Handelsblatt* stated that "quite a number of the 250 students who have so far been trained by the 'Institute for International Solidarity' have advanced to top government positions."* Apparently, Gewandt participated in the opening ceremony of an institute in Blida, Algeria, "which is to train political leaders in African countries."† The expectations that personnel from overseas who have been trained in West German institutions will prove of value to West German companies and state interests is openly voiced in the West German press. The Programme Director of the German Foundation for Developing Countries, in West Berlin, has stated:

". . . on those who have gone through our hands it will be possible to rely to a much larger degree, and it will be possible to launch them into key posts in their countries and to ever and again give them a backing from Germany by supplying scientific material, industrial connections and professional assistance."‡

West Germany has a whole series of additional institutions and agencies which assist the Government to pursue its neo-colonialist aims in the developing countries. It has been estimated that there are more than 250 state, semi-state and private organisations and thirteen ministries in West Germany dealing with such questions, and that between 1956 and 1962 no less than 895 million marks was spent by the Government alone on such bodies and their activities overseas.¶ Particular use is apparently made of "cultural" institutions, the most prominent of these being the Goethe Institute for the Propagation of the German Language and Culture Abroad, with head-

* December 23, 1964.

† *Frankfurter Allgemeine Zeitung*, April 22, 1965.

‡ Dankwortt, Dieter: *On the Psychology of German Development Aid*, Bonn, 1962, p. 163.

¶ See *The Neo-Colonialism of the West German Federal Republic*, published in the German Democratic Republic, 1965, p. 230.

quarters in Munich. Financed by the West German Government to the extent of twenty million marks a year, this
institute now directs all the cultural institutes abroad which
were formerly under the West German Foreign Office, though
the latter still exercises functions of supervision.

In Britain, too, there are a number of agencies and bodies
concerned with sending personnel to the former colonies, and
with training people from the new states. The close connection
between "technical training" and imperialist strategy was
revealed in a letter to *The Times** by Professor Henry Richardson, Visiting Professor at the Faculty of Administrative
Sciences, Middle East Technical University, Ankara, Turkey.
Explaining that this university caters for students throughout
the Middle East, and suggesting ways by which the Ministry
of Overseas Development (whose origins and purposes have
been explained above) can assist, Professor Richardson
explains that the university is "assisted by various countries,
including Britain and the United States, and by such bodies
as O.E.C.D. and CENTO". Clearly, a military bloc such as
CENTO would have no interest in the university unless it was
making a contribution, in one form or another, to the military
objectives of this alliance.

The fact that such institutions as universities can be involved
in the neo-colonialist plans of government is strikingly shown
by the remarkable example of the Michigan State University,
and its role in South Vietnam. In the spring of 1955 the U.S.
Vice-President at that time, Mr. Richard Nixon, allegedly
approached Mr. John Hannah, the President of the Michigan
State University, and asked him to assist in carrying out a
project that had apparently been decided on by the National
Security Council.† Officially the project was to be part of
the International Co-operation Administration programme of
assistance to underdeveloped countries. The "assistance"

---

* November 16, 1964.

† For full details of this connivance of the Michigan State University with
the State Department's plans in South Vietnam, see *How the United States
Got Involved in Vietnam* by Robert Scheer, California, 1965.

proved to be quite bizarre. As Mr. Scheer explains, it was to "fill a special need". This "special need", which involved 54 professors and two hundred Vietnamese assistants, is explained by Mr. Sheer in these words:

"The Geneva Accords had prohibited increases in the strength of either side through the introduction of 'all types of arms' or build-ups in troop strength. The presence of the International Control Commission (made up of nationals of Canada, Poland and India) offered the prospect of unfavourable publicity to the United States if its Military Assistance Advisory Group (M.A.A.G.), United States Operation Mission, or C.I.A. agents operated openly. The Michigan group would serve as 'cover'."

Under this "cover", the Michigan university professors went to work reorganising the police and security forces for Diem, the puppet dictator of South Vietnam. The head of the Michigan State University School of Police Administration, Art Brandstatter, was one of those seconded for this purpose. Under his training programme, Diem's Palace Guard was supplied with guns and ammunition which the Michigan State University professors obtained from the U.S.-M.A.A.G. The old French-trained Sureté type detective force was transformed into a Vietnamese Bureau of Investigation, modelled on the American F.B.I. The police force was turned into a para-military unit, and trained especially to deal with popular uprisings against the Diem dictatorship. To "pacify" the countryside, a 40,000-strong Civil Guard was established. Immigration authorities were given finger-print training, and all government departments were trained in maintaining security dossiers. The monthly records of the project tell of guns, ammunition, vehicles, grenades, handcuffs, and tear-gas equipment passed by the Michigan professors to the United States protegés in South Vietnam. As Mr. Scheer explains, "From 1955 to 1960, the Michigan team had the major responsibility for training, equipping and financing the police apparatus for Diem's state."

Understandably enough, one project head cynically commented: "Knock it out of your head that 99 per cent of university guys are educators—they are all operators."

This is undoubtedly an exaggerated view, but at the same time the Michigan State University project certainly illustrates that where neo-colonialism and plotting against the peoples of the Third World are concerned, there is no end to the various subterfuges which the imperialist powers use. "Not everything is what it seems" would appear to be a golden rule when estimating the role of various Western controlled institutions operating in the developing countries. The C.I.A., in particular, functions in a variety of guises, and utilises many other existing bodies. It has even set up business companies which are, in reality, C.I.A. agencies. This is true, for example, of the Western Enterprises Inc., Taiwan, and the New Asia Trading Company in India. There are several firms in Nigeria, too, which are disguised C.I.A. agencies.

Trade unions are another field in which the C.I.A. is active.*
On his return to the United States, after touring Africa, Mr. Richard Nixon, former U.S. Vice-President, stated: "It is of vital importance that the American Government should closely follow what goes on in the trade union sphere, and that American consular and diplomatic representatives should get to know the trade union leaders of these countries intimately . . ." Explaining the purposes of such activity more specifically, George Cabot Lodge, son of the former U.S. Ambassador to Saigon, has said: "*Our foreign policy cannot be successful* unless it specifically includes and gives priority to the activities of workers' organisations in these vast areas."† Mr. Lodge explains that "many unions (in developing countries) could not afford politically to accept aid from the U.S. Government. It would make them appear to be agents of the United States, which in neutral areas is sometimes inadvisable." He therefore outlines

* See especially Morris, George: *C.I.A. and American Labour*, New York, 1967.

† Lodge, George Cabot: *Spearheads of Democracy—Labour in the Developing Countries*, 1962, New York, p. xii.

a variety of methods and guises through which American finance can be channelled from employers and government bodies via the AFL-CIO, via the International Confederation of Free Trade Unions and its Trade Secretariats, and via different "aid" projects, the funds passing from the U.S. to governments in the Third World which, in their turn, pass the finances on to trade union leaders supporting U.S. policy.

A particular American agency concerned with union matters is the American Institute for Free Labour Development (AIFLD), a body which is largely sponsored and financed by American business interests. On its Board of Trustees and amongst its sponsors are such people as Peter Grace, who has industrial and banking interests in a number of Latin American countries, and Charles Brinckerhoff, a director of the huge Anaconda copper company. Its director, William C. Doherty, has explained "There are many advantages to business involvement in AIFLD. . . . Business support for AIFLD also shows Latin-American workers that not all his businessmen have horns." The AIFLD was particularly prominent in Guyana in 1963, where its involvement in the rioting and hooliganism against the P.P.P. Government headed by Dr. Jagan, was commented on quite freely in the American press.* On the basis of this experience, an Afro-American Labour Centre has been set up for Africa, with similar aims and business backing as the AIFLD which operates mainly in Latin America. A bulletin of the Afro-American Labour Centre, for March, 1965, makes clear one of the main motives in setting up this institution: "It will also encourage labour-management co-operation *to expand American capital investment in the African nations.*"

From all the foregoing it should be apparent that a major agency of American neo-colonialism is the C.I.A. and other bodies connected with the security organs. British, French, West German and other West European intelligence and security services perform a similar service for their respective

* For details, see Jagan, Cheddi: *The West on Trial*, op. cit., pp. 274–304; and Reno, Philip: *The Ordeal of British Guiana*, New York, 1964, pp. 50–57.

Governments. Revelations of C.I.A. plots and conspiracies, successful in some cases, unsuccessful in others, are almost commonplace.* The hand of the C.I.A. was obvious in the overthrow of Mossadeq in Iran (1953), and of the Arbenz Government of Guatemala (1954), as well as in the murder of Lumumba (1960). It was almost certainly present in the 1965 coup against Indonesia, as well as in a number of coups in Latin America.

At the same time, it would be incorrect to advance a kind of "theory of conspiracy" as the sole explanation of the reverses that have taken place in a number of countries in recent years. There have certainly been plots organised by the C.I.A. and it would be unwise to underestimate the activities of this institution or of the intelligence and espionage organisations of other imperialist powers; but such agencies can only operate within certain given conditions. They cannot remove a government unless they have something to instal in its place; and those who are hoisted into power in this way, even when they govern by absolute terror and repression, need to base themselves on specific social forces. The intelligence agencies of the West have for years been actively engaged in plotting against the Soviet Union and, in more recent years, against other socialist countries. If they have scored no striking successes here, it is because the strata and social classes (i.e. landlords and capitalists, together with petty-bourgeois forces allied to these circles) no longer exist as classes, or have been greatly diminished and are firmly controlled by socialist states led by revolutionary parties.

In the new states of Africa and Asia, however, as well as in the Latin American countries, there are internal forces with which neo-colonialism can ally itself. Feudal landlords anxious to maintain or regain their former economic status and privileged position in society; traders and speculators who fear

* See, for example, Wise, David and Ross, Thomas B.: *The Invisible Government*, New York, 1964; London, 1965. See also the widespread revelations of C.I.A. activity amongst organisations of students, lawyers, journalists, trade unions, etc., which followed the *Ramparts* exposure of March 1967.

the advent of socialism and wish to continue as middlemen of the big international monopolies; sections of the new élite, bribed and corrupted, in a hurry to grow rich on the fruits of office before the undernourished millions demand a reckoning; all the hangers-on of capitalism, the *nouveaux riches* the career boys and diplomats, the police chiefs and generals, all the nauseating imitators of the most decadent and parasitical classes in the West, described with such withering scorn by Frantz Fanon as "a sort of little greedy caste, avid and voracious, with the mind of a huckster, only too glad to accept the dividends that the former colonial power hands out to it."* It is through these social forces that the Western powers influence affairs in the countries of the Third World; and an essential aim of neo-colonialism is precisely to nurture and mould such strata. As Amilcar Cabral, leader of the people of "Portuguese" Guinea has explained,† one of the essential aims of neo-colonialism "is to create a false bourgeoisie to put a brake on the revolution, and to enlarge the possibilities of the petty bourgeoisie as a neutraliser of the revolution." And in pursuit of this aim, the imperialist powers utilise all the forms of neo-colonialism.

Particular attention is paid to the whole field of ideas and sources of information. In most countries of the Third World the means of communication—press, radio, television, education—are largely influenced by, and often in the hands of representatives of the Western Powers. In Africa, for example, there has been a big move in by big Western press monopolies in the past few years, Lord Thomson and Cecil King in particular assuming a commanding position in a number of countries.‡ The same kind of control is to be seen in Asia and Latin

* Fanon, Frantz: *The Damned*, Paris, 1963., p. 141.

† Amilcar Cabral is leader of the PAIGC—Parti Africain de l'Indépendence de la Guinee 'Portugaise' et des Iles du Cap-Vert—which is leading the struggle in that region, and which has already liberated half the territory. The quotation cited comes from a series of lectures he delivered on May 1–3, 1964, at Treviglio, in Italy, at a seminar convened by the Frantz Fanon Centre of Milan.

‡ See Ainslie, Rosalynde: *The Press in Africa*, London, 1966, for details.

America, although not quite to the same extent as in Africa. Through these propaganda media, and making use of additional institutions such as libraries, information centres, social and economic institutes, and so on, the Western powers spread a number of ideas and conceptions which hold back the full liberation of the former colonies, tie them more closely to imperialism, and encourage them to accept capitalism rather than socialism.

The peoples are constantly told that they need "Western know-how", that they "cannot do without foreign capital", that they should not nationalise foreign enterprises, and that they should base themselves on agriculture and tourism rather than on industry, which is sometimes dismissed as mere "prestige building". A special role is played by the spread of anti-Communist ideas which are designed to divide the national movement, to isolate the new states from the socialist countries, and to discourage the people from adopting the ideas of scientific socialism, of Marxism. Sometimes, in order to confuse the people, the very process of building capitalism goes ahead under false slogans of particular types of "socialism", such as "African socialism", or "Islamic socialism".

Thus in Kenya, for example, the launching of the programme of "African socialism" was immediately followed by an attack on the left-wing forces led by Oginga Odinga, and was quickly revealed as a programme for African capitalism in alliance with American and European monopoly firms.* A Fabian review of the official Kenya booklet on "African Socialism" concluded that the Kenya government had "opted for the capitalist direction of economic development."†

Military treaties, alliances and bases are also an essential weapon in the armoury of neo-colonialism. The United States alone has some 1,234 bases in 44 countries, apart from those of other imperialist powers. The purpose of these bases is not hidden. "Bases are absolutely essential in stopping local

* See Cox, Idris: *Socialist Ideas in Africa*, London, 1966, pp. 77/8.
† McCauslan, Patrick: *Venture*, September 1965.

wars or 'wars of national liberation' ".* "Military bases
provide the military foundations for political intervention in
times of peace; they nearly always function as centres of prestige, power and cultural importance of their owners, thus
enabling the exertion of pressure and the establishment and
enforcement of interests in the surrounding regions—even
without the direct use of military force."†

In addition to bases and military alliances, neo-colonialism
relies very heavily on its contacts with military personnel. The
provision of arms provides the opportunity to send instructors.
Military alliances or agreements are accompanied by the
sending of military advisers and liaison personnel. Military
academies, such as Sandhurst and Camberley in Britain, St.
Cyr in France, and Fort Bragg, the counter-guerrilla centre in
the United States, all provide the opportunity for the Western
powers to make acquaintance with the military leaders or
future leaders of the new states. In this way they are able to
sort out the sheep from the goats, to select those who are most
likely to prove corrupt and pliable. It is no accident that in
most cases the reactionary military groups which have come
to power in recent years in Africa and Asia have been composed mainly of personnel trained in Western military
academies.‡

A striking example is Colonel A. A. Afrifa, one of the
leaders of the coup d'état in Ghana last year. In his recent
book,¶ Col. Afrifa reveals how at Sandhurst he became a loyal
supporter of imperialism, completely caught up by the mystique
of the Commonwealth and the flattering treatment he was

---

* Kintner, William R.: *National Security. Political, Military and Economic
Strategies in the Decade Ahead*, New York, 1963, p. 391.

† Ratcliffe, A. L.: *Wehrkunde*, Munich, No. 6, 1957. (This is the official
journal of the War Ministry of the Federal Republic of Germany.)

‡ These academies are not always successful. Turcios Lima was trained at
Fort Bragg. On his return to Guatemala he led an army revolt against
governmental tyranny, and became leader of the guerrilla forces. In 1966 he
joined the Communist Party, a few months before his assassination at the
early age of 25.

¶ Afrifa, A. A.: *The Ghana Coup*, London, 1966, pp. 49–52.

given during his training in Britain. He describes Sandhurst as "a wonderful and mysterious institution with traditions going back to 1802. One cannot appreciate its mystery unless one experiences Sandhurst. . . . No one cared whether one was a prince, lord, commoner, foreigner, Muslim or black man. There were quite a number of lords and princes at Sandhurst. Everyone was treated according to his own merits. . . . The food at Sandhurst was good; I loved the companionship of people of identical calling, and the English breakfast."

After all this, it is not surprising that he should write: "Now I look back on Sandhurst with nostalgia. It is one of the greatest institutions in the world. Through its doors have passed famous generals, kings and rulers." The effect of this Sandhurst "brain-washing" is also to be seen in Col. Afrifa's attitude towards Britain and the Commonwealth. "I have been trained in the United Kingdom as a soldier, and I am ever prepared to fight alongside my friends in the United Kingdom in the same way as Canadians and Australians will do. How could we be friends belonging to the Commonwealth and stay out in time of Commonwealth adversity, and when this great Union is in danger?". Thus does neo-colonialism seek out and mould its men.

ECONOMIC POLICIES OF NEO-COLONIALISM

At the centre of all the activities of neo-colonialism lies its economic policies. These are directed to assisting the profit-making functions of the big monopolies, to providing the Western powers with the necessary economic power in the new states so as to be able to wield political influence over the governments there, and to foster a certain growth of capitalism in order to nourish a class which will co-operate with imperialism and hinder the advance to socialism. All these three inter-linked objectives lie behind the economic policies of the Western powers towards the countries of the Third World.

In a brief introductory study such as this it is not possible to make a comprehensive examination of all the economic

institutions and forms of activity practised by Western Governments and Western monopolies in Africa, Asia and Latin
America; nor is it possible to provide a complete picture of the
results of these policies. But certain essential features should be
noted, for they help to throw a light on the general phenomenon of neo-colonialism.

One of the aims of neo-colonialism is to retain essentially the
same economic relationship between imperialism and the
developing countries as has existed up until now. Some
changes, as has already been indicated, will be encouraged in
order to set these countries on to the path of capitalist development. This will mean some modification in existing structures,
a degree of industrial development, some changes in land
tenure and agrarian systems—but essentially, in the plans of
neo-colonialism, these territories are to remain as producers of
raw materials (some degree of processing to be allowed), providing minerals, industrial crops, and foodstuffs for Western
industry and commerce, and acting as markets for Western
manufactured goods. This pattern of economic relationships,
it is hoped, will also serve to protect imperialist political and
strategic interests since it will keep the developing countries
economically weak and dependent on imperialism. "He who
pays the piper calls the tune", and especially is this likely to
be so when the particular local government is composed of
feudal, bourgeois and petty-bourgeois strata who accept that
their countries remain weak semi-capitalist dependencies
rather than strike out in the direction of socialism.

Western investments, loans, trading policies and "aid"
schemes are all directed to the aim of keeping these territories
as primary-producing hinterlands of imperialism which import
the bulk of their machinery and manufactured goods from the
metropolitan countries.

Private investments, for example, are directed mainly to
mining and plantations, which are sources of huge profits for
imperialism. Most U.S. investment, for example, points out
Richard J. Barber,* is "in the extractive industries, oil, copper,

* Barber, Richard J.: See *The New Republic*, April 30, 1966.

iron ore, cobalt, rubber, bauxite, uranium and other minerals.
... Very little capital is invested in manufacturing facilities,*
with the result that the underdeveloped countries fail to
acquire the skill necessary for development. As things stand,
the emerging nations are caught in a serious bind: they sell
their oil and minerals under conditions distinctly favourable
to the buyers and purchase finished goods on terms favourable
to sellers, with their predicaments aggravated by the ocean
shipping conferences which are prone to rig transport rates in
a fashion that still further disadvantages the new nations."

Such investments are, of course, immensely profitable for
these big firms. In fact, available figures for the United States
show that the net income from these investments each year
exceeds the net outflow in the form of new investments. For
the years 1950 to 1961, the total net direct investment capital
outflow from the United States was 13,708 million dollars, while
the total income from these investments was 23,204 million
dollars.† A report of the American National Industrial Conference Board, which continues the examination of American
overseas investment beyond 1961, states that with the exception of a single year "profits repatriated from direct foreign
investments have exceeded the new capital outflows in every
year since 1950. In 1964, for example, foreign investments
returned $3·6 billion to the U.S.A., compared with a new
capital outflow of $2·3 billion—for a net gain to the U.S. of

* This was well illustrated in an outstanding paper on Neo-Colonialism
read by Ali Yata, General Secretary of the Moroccan Communist Party, at
a special seminar on *Africa—National and Social Revolution*, held in Cairo,
October 1966. Ali Yata stated that out of 1,629 million dollars invested by
the United States in Africa in 1964, only 225 million were for manufacturing
industries—and of this total 192 million were invested in the Republic of
South Africa. This left only 33 million dollars for the rest of the continent.
In other words, only about 2 per cent of U.S. investment in Africa (apart
from the industrialised, white-dominated South Africa) went on manufacturing; and in relation to the population this meant only about seven dollars
per head per year.

† Table compiled by Baran and Sweezy from *Survey of Current Business*,
U.S. Department of Commerce. Quoted in Roy, Ajit: *Economics and Politics
of U.S. Foreign Aid*, Calcutta, 1966, p. 51.

$1·3 billion. In 1965, preliminary Administration figures indicate that the return from the U.S. direct investments was slightly over $4·0 billion compared to about $3·0 billion of fresh capital sent abroad."

These figures in themselves reveal only part of the truth, since they state *net* gains. Gross profits from these investments are now estimated to be running at over $8,000 million a year. Most of this is derived from the more industrially developed countries (Canada, Europe, Australia), but a substantial amount comes from the developing countries. For Britain, too, overseas investments are a lucrative source of profit for the big monopolies. By 1965, overseas interest, profits and dividends amounted to £1,003 million.* Again, as in the case of the United States, most of this comes from the more developed countries, but a considerable share comes from the newly independent countries. For the period 1956–62, it has been estimated that the western monopolies exported over 30,000 million dollars to 56 developing countries, but received back in interest and profits 15,000 million dollars. In other words, in a mere six years they derived benefits equivalent to half of their export.

It is therefore evident that whatever may be the benefits to the developing countries from foreign investments, the benefits to the investors are far greater. In fact, the above figures indicate that foreign investment, far from being a means of assisting developing countries, is mainly a form of transferring wealth from the Third World to the imperialist states, while making it easier for the latter to increase their economic stranglehold on the former.

Foreign loans (usually through State agencies) serve the same purposes. First, there is the question of their direction. Foreign loans, where they go to governments in the Third World, are usually ear-marked for improving the infrastructure —for building roads, ports, airfields. These are not entirely useless for the developing country but the reasons why foreign State loans are used in this way are that such developments

* *Balance of Payments Report*, 1966.

require the expenditure of vast sums for which there is not the quick and large return to attract private investors; the construction of such lines of communication is not without its military-strategic purposes; and the new facilities make possible a more speedy and large-scale export of raw materials to the imperialist centres. Thus, the iron ore of Fort Gouraud, Mauretania, of Mount Nimba, Liberia, and of Swaziland, is being heavily exploited by foreign monopolies. In each case, the governments are building railways and port installations to carry away the ore—in the first two cases to the West, in the last-named to Japan. The same has happened with the rich iron ore of Venezuela, which is being exploited by U.S. companies.

A second feature of the loans (and this is often connected with various "aid" schemes), is that the lending country usually stipulates that they must be used neither to construct heavy industry, nor to assist the State sector of the economy at the expense of private enterprise. That the open encouragement of private capitalist development is their aim in the developing countries is not hidden by official circles in the United States. "It is a basic policy of the ICA (International Co-operation Administration) to employ U.S. assistance to aid-receiving countries in such a way as will encourage the private sector of their economy."* Secretary of State, Dean Rusk, has himself declared: "We are increasing our efforts to stimulate the private sector in the developing countries and increase the role of U.S. private enterprise in our assistance programme."† What this can mean in terms of a particular country is illustrated by Liberia. In the past quarter of a century, the big American rubber firm, Firestone, has taken $160 million worth of rubber out of Liberia; in return the Liberian Government has received a paltry $8 million. The average net profit made by this American company is three times the entire Liberian revenue.‡

* Krause, Walter: *Economic Development—Underdeveloped World and the American Interest*, San Francisco, 1961, p. 407.
† *Department of State Bulletin*, Washington, April 18, 1966.
‡ Nkrumah, Kwame: op. cit., p. 66.

The third feature of foreign loans from the West is their high interest rates. The result has been the placing of an impossible burden on the developing countries, to such an extent that many of them can no longer "afford" to "receive" a loan. The high interest charges (often 6 to 7 per cent, and with the capital to be repaid in a relatively short time, too), combined with the conditions under which the loans are made, and their use for undertakings which do not produce large or quick returns, means that the receiving country has to spend more and more of its gross national product not for its own development but in paying overseas money-lenders for their pound of flesh. World Bank figures for 1962 showed that 71 countries of Asia, Africa and Latin America owed foreign debts to the tune of $27,000 million, on which they paid interest and service charges of $5,000 million. In May, 1963, Mr. George Thomson, Minister for Foreign Affairs in the British Government, said that 28 per cent of British "aid" goes to pay back the interest on former aid. On January 7, 1966, the *Financial Times* wrote that "between now and the early 1970's the under-developed countries as a whole are due to repay from a quarter to a half of their foreign debt. And as this is estimated to be in the region of £9,800 million, it is not difficult to imagine what this is going to mean for countries whose combined annual export earnings do not usually amount to much more than £13,000 million."

The latest figures show quite clearly that the amount pumped out from the underdeveloped countries in profits and interest on loans rises year by year, and steadily becomes an increasing proportion of the total amount of "aid" provided. Thus a recent report of the Secretary General to the United Nations Conference on Trade and Development (UNCTAD) showed that the indebtedness of the developing countries had increased from 9,000 million dollars in 1955 to 33,000 million in 1964. This means that over half of the total international flow of financial "aid" to the developing countries is now offset by interest on their debts, and by the outflow of profits and dividends to the foreign monopoly firms which have invested in their countries.

The further unfolding of this trend will put the developing countries in an impossible position. The President of the International Bank for Reconstruction and Development, George D. Woods, has pointed out that "the underdeveloped countries as a whole must now devote more than a tenth of their foreign-exchange earnings to debt service . . . These payments are continuing to rise at an accelerating rate, and in a little more than fifteen years, on present form, *would offset the inflow completely*."* (Emphasis added.)

Loans from imperialist countries have clearly become a means of placing developing countries further in thrall and making them utterly dependent on Western Governments and banking institutions.

Robbery through profits and interest on loans is not the only burden which the developing countries have to bear. There is a third channel through which the wealth of the developing countries is drained away, and that is the unfair price relationship between the prices of their primary goods exports and the prices of the machinery and manufactured goods which they import from the West.

A special U.N. study in 1949 showed that between 1897 and 1938 the average prices of primary products fell by approximately a third in relation to those of manufactured goods. A further U.N. study (*Economic Problems*, No. 600, June 20, 1959) points out that the increase in prices of industrial goods and the decline in prices of raw materials represented a loss in import capacity for underdeveloped countries of approximately "the equivalent of six years of loans to underdeveloped countries by the International Bank for Reconstruction and Development, on the basis of 1956–7 prices". Pierre Moussa† calculates that, on the basis that the export of basic products by the non-industrialised areas of the world amounts to about £25 billion, "an adjustment of prices of 14 per cent would therefore suffice to increase the annual income of the *Tiers-Monde* (Third World) by £3.5 billion, the present total of all

* *Foreign Affairs*, January 1966, pp. 211–212.
† *Les Nations Proletaires*: Paris 1960, p. 20.

public aid to underdeveloped countries". A United Nations Report in 1961 (*International Economic Assistance to the Less Developed Countries*) reveals that between 1953–5 and 1957–9 the loss through the worsening in terms of trade for underdeveloped countries was nearly twice the total amount of public aid funds these countries received.

Between the years 1954–1962, the production and export of cocoa in Nigeria went up by 120 per cent—yet for more than doubling her export of cocoa, Nigeria received only £29 million, as against £30 million in 1954. If she had received in 1962 the same price for her cocoa as she had received in 1954, she would have been paid £70 million—in other words, she was robbed of £41 million. But the robbery does not end there, because during this same period the prices of the machines and the manufactured goods she had to import went up considerably.

Similarly, in 1952, Ghana was being paid £467 a ton for her cocoa. After independence in 1957 she estimated her planned economic development on the assumption that she could rely on the modest price of £200 a ton for several years. In fact, the large western importers had more or less given such an assurance. By 1965, however, the price was down to £85 a ton. This played havoc with Ghana's economic development and was one of the causes of the economic difficulties and discontent which were part of the background to the coup against President Nkrumah.

When one considers that Ghana received £85·5 million in 1954/5 for 210,000 tons of cocoa, compared with only £77 million in 1964/5 for 590,000 tons, and after spending £30 million on fighting cocoa disease (swollen shoot, pests, etc.), one can begin to realise how much the developing countries suffer through the ability of the Western powers to dominate the capitalist market and to manipulate prices in their own favour and to the detriment of the Third World.

These examples indicate the problem of the under-developed countries. Over a period of years the prices of the raw materials —whether minerals or cash crops—tend to fall or to rise very slowly and always to fluctuate, in comparison with the prices of the manufactured goods and especially machinery, which they have to import.

The amount of this robbery is so great that the gap between the western industrialist countries and the countries of the Third World grows wider and wider. For Latin America, according to the International Monetary Fund, the losses resulting from the non-equivalent exchange forced on it by the United States amounted for the period 1951–1962, to some 20,500 million dollars. For Africa, Professor Dumont has noted : "From 1955 to 1959 export prices went down 15 per cent, entailing a loss to tropical Africa of 600 million dollars, twice the annual amount of foreign aid."* For all the developing countries it was estimated at the United Nations Conference on Trade and Development in 1965 that, at the present rate of robbery arising from the unequal exchange, the total loss in the year 1970 for these territories would be 7,000 million dollars (£2,800 million).

To present the problem in another way we give the following table :

UNEQUAL EXCHANGE

To buy 1 ton imported steel—	1951	1961	Increase
Ghana (lbs cocoa)	202	571	283%
Brazil (lbs coffee)	158	380	240%
Malaya (lbs rubber)	132	441	334%

Thus the amount of steel these countries imported has had to be paid for by increasing quantities of their main exports. This is sheer robbery.

This obvious cause of difficulty for the developing countries and the necessity to provide them with more equitable trading relations has led them to press for fair trading rather than aid. The Western powers have replied by constantly opposing every measure which would make things easier for them.

When the United Nations Conference on Trade and Development took place in Geneva between March and June 1965, 121

* Dumont, René: op. cit., p. 123.

countries were present including 77 countries of the Third World. The *Financial Times* commented at that time that Britain, in common with the United States and other Western countries, was "opposed to the Conference from the start".

The voting at the Conference certainly bears this out. The Conference voted on fifteen General Principles and thirteen Special Principles. On issue after issue, we find the overwhelming majority of the countries, including the representatives of Asia, Africa and Latin America, together with the Soviet Union and other socialist countries, sometimes joined by some of the smaller west European countries, voting in favour of progressive resolutions against the opposition or abstention of a handful of countries, mainly the major Western powers and invariably including both the United States and the United Kingdom. A specific proposal dealing with the loss to the developing countries resulting from the unequal price relationship, Special Principle Number 7, urged that "extra measures should be taken to correct falls in prices in primary products in order to protect primary producers from loss of income." Eighty-five countries voted for this proposal, but thirteen voted against, including the United States and Britain.

While the industrially developed Western powers have, over recent years, taken more from the developing countries in profits, in interest on loans and capital repayment, and through the advantages they gain as a result of the unequal price relationships, the amounts allocated by them in various so-called "aid" schemes has steadily declined. The combined total economic aid of the O.E.C.D. countries (thirteen West European countries, together with Canada and the United States) dropped from £2,282 million in 1963 to £2,222 million in 1964.

The United States, which accounts for about 60 per cent of the total, made the biggest cuts. United States official "foreign aid" schemes have dropped from an annual average of £2,000 million in the late 1950's to roughly £1,200 million for the current year—which is about 40 per cent of the current profits from overseas investment. This "aid", includes military assistance to "countries bordering on the Soviet Union and China". This year's projected £1,200 million is to be divided between £880 million for economic purposes, and £327 million for military aid. The latter figure, however, is irrespective of the war in Vietnam and of other military actions. The journal *Fortune* has calculated that the Vietnam war in 1966 was costing the United States £5,480 million a year, and that in the next fiscal year it would be £7,600 million.* The purposes of American aid, and the extent to which military and political considerations determine its scope and direction, are openly admitted in the United States. Commenting on the report of the Clay Committee which had been appointed by the late President Kennedy to examine U.S. foreign aid, the London *Times* wrote editorially:

> "American aid is not just aid, but part of foreign policy. The Committee calculated that 44 per cent of American aid was military and economic support for allied countries bordering the communist bloc, and if the sums spent in Vietnam and Laos are included, the share of total appropriations comes to 72 per cent."†

In some instances, the proportion of the "aid" which is actually spent on undertakings of economic value to the recipient country is almost negligible, and sometimes completely so. For example, in the case of Laos, a report appearing in the *Tribune des Nations* in 1957, stated "Official American aid to Laos is running at $74 million a year. This aid is apportioned as follows: 7 million dollars for the police and state security organisations, 7 million for the administration, 50 million for an army of 25,000 men and another 10 million for the keep of 250 American advisers and experts." A quick calculation shows that the above items take up the whole of the 74 million dollars. Not a single dollar is left for economic development, neither industrial nor agricultural. What makes

* *See Financial Times*, May 20, 1966.
† March 28, 1963.

it even more damaging—and the same applies generally to other countries receiving this form of "aid"—is that the money is used to prop up political systems which resist the kind of social changes which would enable the people to build up independent economies and overcome their under-development.

The total proposed American "foreign aid" figure for 1966-7 of £1,200 million is the lowest for the whole post-war period. When one takes into account, too, that of the £880 million allocated for economic purposes, twenty per cent is to go to Saigon—i.e. for the war, the amount allocated for specific *economic* aid is also the lowest in this period. Apart from the increasing amounts going for military purposes, the pattern of American "aid" also shows an increasing tendency to turn from grants to loans. In 1959–61, the share of loans in total aid did not exceed an average of 36 per cent. In 1962–4, it went up to 64 per cent, and in the 1955–6 fiscal year it is as high as 69 per cent.* The same trend can be seen with British "aid". For 1966-7, the target is £225 million—less than a tenth of the combined "invisible earnings" for 1965. The figure is 0·66 per cent of the national income, although the official policy of the British Labour Government was to allocate one per cent to aid. In 1963, the proportion of British "bilateral aid" in the form of loans was 40 per cent, by 1964 it was 66 per cent, and in 1965 77 per cent.†

There are other ways in which "aid" schemes benefit the donor. Invariably a high proportion of the funds loaned is used on purchases by the recipient from the donor at prices higher than those prevailing on the world market. A report of Dr. Franz Pick, who visited Pakistan in 1963, pointed out that U.S. assistance is a veiled form of what he termed "self-financing", and was, in fact, "a subsidy to the U.S. domestic indus-

* See *Summary Report of a Study on Loan Terms, Debt Burden and Development.* Agency for International Development, Department of State, April 1965, Cited by Y. Yelutin and M. Petrov, *International Affairs*, p. 51, Moscow, June 1966.

† See Cox, Idris: "*World Hunger and Economic 'Aid'*", *Marxism Today*, July 1966, p. 213.

try".* His study revealed that 90 per cent of the $4,500 million advanced annually by the United States to developing countries is spent in the United States itself. In summarising this study, the *Financial Times* Karachi correspondent commented: "Certainly, over 90 per cent of the aid that the U.S. offers to Pakistan as loans is ploughed back to the U.S. economy in the form of commodity purchases made in the U.S.—at higher than world market prices—consultants' fees, salaries of experts, freight and insurance charges, and interest and loan servicing charges."† In the 1966-7 "aid" programme of the United States, one third of the 500 million dollars allocated for agriculture is for the purchase of American fertilisers.‡

Thus, in a variety of ways the imperialist powers, even after they no longer wield direct state power in colonial territories, continue to exploit their manpower and resources. In fact, the extent of robbery increases. The newly independent states, standing on shaky legs and taking their first hesitant steps to construct independent and balanced economies, find themselves confronted not solely by one imperialist power as hitherto during the days of colonial rule but by a series of imperialist states, each of which is anxious to obtain the maximum profit. In particular, they are faced with the United States, the most economically powerful and ruthless of the imperialist states.

It is a specific feature of neo-colonialism that, in addition to providing new opportunities for each imperialist power, it also makes possible their *joint* exploitation of the developing countries. The term "collective colonialism" has been used to describe these new joint efforts. Sometimes they take the form of the establishment of giant financial consortia by international monopolies, such as the Iron Ore Company of Mekambo, comprising French, West German, Italian, Dutch, Belgian and American capital, which is operating in Gabon; Miferma (British, French, West German and Italian capital) exploiting the iron ore of Mauretania; Fria (American, British, French and Swiss capital) exploiting the bauxite of Guinea.

Collective colonialism has also resulted in the setting up of specific international bodies, financial agencies and arrangements, such as the International Monetary Fund, the International Bank of Reconstruction and Development, the International Development Association, the International Fund for Economic Development, and the International Finance Corporation, all of which are dominated by U.S. banks.

These are forms intended to hide the face of the "Ugly American" whose image is becoming very much tarnished in the Third World. One enthusiastic advocate* of these neo-colonialist methods favours aid for Africa "on a bilateral basis or on a special consortium basis" within the framework of a special "flexible multilateral organisation". Mr. Rivkin makes no secret of the political aim behind this new form of tying Africa to the West. In fact, he blandly explains that this proposal for a new multilateral form of providing "aid" should "make it easier for independent African states to accept free world assistance without exposing themselves to the charge . . . of seeming to exchange one colonial overlord (i.e. the former metropole) for another (i.e. the United States)".

Neo-colonialism is not only a matter of relations between imperialist powers and particular developing countries, but often produces forms of exploitation for entire regions, such as the U.S.-sponsored Alliance for Progress for Latin America, and the European Common Market and its relationship with the "associated" African States.

The experience of the eighteen African associated states of the European Common Market fully exposes the extent to which the Market is used as a device to hold back economic development in Africa in the interests of big European monopolies. Despite the claim that the Common Market would provide a good outlet for African products, and better prices for their raw materials exports, the associated states are having to struggle to maintain their markets in West Europe, and are

* Rivkin, Arnold: *The Politics of African Development External Aid*; speech to the Economic Society of Ghana, reproduced in the Society's monthly journal, *The Economic Bulletin*, Vol. 3, No. 11, November 1959, pp. 18–19.

faced, at the same time, with an ever-increasing gap between the prices of their exports and those of the goods they import from the European Common Market countries.

This was strikingly revealed in recent speeches made in December 1966 by President Diori Hamani of Niger to the Common Market Commission in Brussels, and to the Parliamentary Commission of the Euro-African Association at Abidjan, Ivory Coast.* Referring to "the catastrophic effect on the revenues of developing countries in general and of African countries in particular" of the drop on the world market of the prices of raw materials simultaneously with the constantly rising prices of manufactured articles and capital goods exported by the industrialised countries, he gave this significant example. The exchange value of a ton of cocoa exported in 1960 was sufficient to import into Cameroun 2,700 metres of unbleached material or 1,200 kilos of cement. By 1965, the same quantity of cocoa was sufficient for only 800 metres of cloth or 450 kilos of cement. President Diori Hamani added that although Common Market imports from associated African countries rose between 1963 and 1965 by 66 per cent (from 6,197,879 tons to 10,289,300 tons), their value rose by only 17 per cent (from 833 million dollars to 972 million).

While prices of their exports to the European Common Market tend to fall, the associated states do not find it easier to secure entry for their goods into West European markets. On the contrary, they often find themselves faced with particularly high special consumer taxes, which militate against their selling their commodities. These include the 180 per cent tax on green coffee in West Germany, and 148 per cent tax on cocoa in Italy. Some of these taxes even reach as high as 250 per cent. This helps to explain why, despite the low prices they place on their exports, African associated countries find that their sales in the Market countries are not rising as fast as those from other non-Market countries. The President of the European Common Market Commission, Dr. Hallstein,

* *Perspectives Nigeriennes*, January 1967.

stated in a speech in Amsterdam on February 4, 1964, that between 1958 (when the Common Market first began to function) and 1964, trade with the associated countries rose by 28 per cent, while for Latin American countries it increased by 50 per cent.

Association with the European Common Market also threatens the new, struggling industries of these African states. Formally speaking, the Rome Treaty allows these states to put up protective tariffs to safeguard their industries. The only difficulty is that measures of this kind have to be sanctioned by the Common Market Commission, which is composed of the European Common Market powers busily engaged in trying to expand the export of their manufactures and capital goods into Africa. The associated states, under the July 20th 1963 Yaoundé Convention, were able to obtain some tariff reductions for their exports of raw materials, but if non-Associated countries attempt to export processed or partly made-up commodities they are faced with much higher tariffs.* In the face of such discrimination, non-associated states are striving to secure entry into the Market in the hope of finding better opportunities for selling their products.

The Development Fund, set up by the European Common Market ostensibly to assist the economic growth of the associated African states, has, in fact, become an obstacle to such advance. In the first five years, 1958–62, some £200 million was allocated to the fund. Spread over fifty million people in the then sixteen associated states, the sum to be spent over five years was sufficient only for a halfpenny a head per day. By December 31, 1962, when the term of the first five years had expired, less than 63 per cent of the funds for development had been spent. Apart from the insufficient amount allocated for development, the control of it is in the hands of

* Duty on cocoa beans is 5·4 per cent, on powdered cocoa it is 22 per cent while for chocolate it is 30 per cent. Peanuts and palmnuts are duty free whereas on peanut oil and palmoil the duty is between 9 and 15 per cent. Natural cotton may be exported without duty, but on cotton fabrics there is a 20 per cent duty.

the Common Market powers themselves. As a result most of the money goes on infrastructure and agriculture rather than on basic industrialisation. "The Fund authorities spend the money first and foremost in the interests of foreign capital".*

When the Upper Volta suggested utilising a portion of the Funds for piping oil and natural gas from the Sahara fields to West Africa, in order to assist African industrial development, this was rejected. The same fate has met almost every other proposal put forward by the associated states. By January 1, 1962, of two hundred projects submitted by the African states, more than half had been rejected outright, and work had begun on only six, totalling about £600,000. For the period 1963 to 1967 the Development Fund will have over £260 million. Nearly one third of this is for agriculture. Over 80 per cent of the funds to be allocated are to be handed out in the form of grants. This may appear, at first sight, to be very generous. But the aim of these funds is that they should be used to pave the way for private enterprise. A statement of the Economic and Social Committee of the European Common Market makes this quite clear:

"In view of the importance of private capital investment for industrialising associated countries and of the difficulty of an exact assessment of the political risks incurred in investing capital in those countries, the committee considers it necessary to offer a security restricted exclusively to political risk ... Moreover, non-repayable grants should largely be used for the infrastructure so as to attract private capital."†

By the end of 1965, about 30 per cent of the Fund for the five-year period had been distributed. So once again, it would appear that the substantial sum announced is, in part, intended as a carrot. As *The Economist* has commented cynically: "This kind of money is enough to keep the associated states generally friendly for the present towards Europe." And

* *African Trade and Development*, September 1962, p. 13.

† Bulletin of the European Economic Community, Brussels, April 1966, p. 49.

if they do not remain "friendly", they have been warned what to expect by the Common Market Council of Ministers which, according to the minutes of their meeting on December 18, 1962, declared:

"Should any of the associated countries take measures designed to menace the friendly relations between that country and the EEC or any of their member states, the Council of Ministers will consider the situation and decide what measures should be adopted under the convention."*

ALLIANCE FOR PROGRESS FOR LATIN AMERICA

The U.S. sponsored Alliance for Progress for Latin America has equally proved to be a means of increasing the exploitation of a continent in the interests of foreign capital. For decades, Latin America has been a major source of profit for the big U.S. monopolies. Up to the end of the first world war, these firms were concerned to establish their control in Latin America—and the Marines were always at their disposal for this purpose. Capital exports in this period were relatively small, since a modest investment in mining or plantations yielded extraordinarily large profits. After 1920 the big hunt for oil began. Rockefeller's Standard Oil Company pushed its way into Venezuela, Colombia and Mexico. Wars were fought—the Chaco War between Bolivia and Paraguay, and the war between Peru and Ecuador—in order to oust British oil interests and make Latin America an exclusive hinterland for Standard Oil.

It was after 1945, however, that the major increase in U.S. investments took place in Latin America, and this was even more so after 1950. The total value of U.S. investments in Latin America rose from 2,721 million dollars in 1943 to 4,445 million in 1950, and to 8,932 million in 1964. These investments were directed particularly to oil, and to the new manufacturing industries which have been established since

* Cited by Brendel, Gerhard: "Economic Relations of EEC Countries to African Associations" *German Foreign Policy*, No. 5, 1966, Berlin, p. 360.

the end of the second world war. By 1964 oil and manufacturing accounted for 61 per cent of U.S. direct investment in Latin America.

This big economic push by the United States was accompanied by a new series of political interventions intended to produce regimes amenable to American policies. After 1948, as was noted earlier in this book, the attack on the democratic movements in Latin America was launched. In one country after another military coups took place, and the era of the "gorillas" began. It has been estimated that in the first fifteen years after the war there were no less than sixty putsches in Latin America.

The victory of the Cuban revolution in 1959 ushered in a new stage in the history of the Latin American people. The overthrow of the American-backed Batista dictatorship on the very doorstep of the United States (in modern military terms), the defeat of the invaders at the Bay of Pigs in 1961, America's climb down after the missile crisis of 1962, and the radical economic and social changes introduced in the new Cuba, all had a most powerful impact throughout the Latin American continent.

The U.S. State Department had to do some hard thinking; and in 1961, two years after the Cuban revolution, a year after "Africa Year", a year after the formation of the South Vietnam National Liberation Front, and in the same year as the Bay of Pigs fiasco, the Peace Corps was formed, and Washington summoned the Latin American governments to a conference at Punta del Este, Uruguay, which gave birth to the "Alliance for Progress."*

This was, in every way, an alliance for neo-colonialism. Its aim was to carry through, over a period of ten years, 1961–70, a "peaceful revolution" in order to avoid a real revolution which would end United States economic and political domi-

---

* Richard Bissell, a leading C.I.A. figure, who is reported to have masterminded the Bay of Pigs invasion, was made a chief aide for the Alliance, to study how its funds should be used. (See Gerassi, John: *The Great Fear in Latin America*, New York, 1965, p. 279).

nation over Latin America. It was intended to introduce agrarian reform, and to establish some elements of "representative democracy", the stranglehold of feudalism being weakened and replaced by a stunted, halfway form of capitalism. To realise this programme, a decision was taken to allocate a sum of 2,000 million dollars a year, comprising 1,100 million from the United States budget, and 300 million equally from private United States investors, from international financial bodies, and from investors in West Europe and Japan. It was intended that Latin American goods would find suitable markets at improved and stable prices. Scientific and technical aid, with the assistance of Peace Corps personnel, was also envisaged as part of the programme.

Supporters of the Alliance for Progress have themselves revealed its real purposes. Dean Rusk has written that the Alliance "rests on the concept that this Hemisphere is part of Western Civilisation which we are pledged to defend." Teodoro Moscoso, former U.S. Ambassador to Venezuela, later head of the Latin American programme of the Agency for International Development, and then chief of the Alliance for Progress, has stated quite candidly: "In supporting the Alliance, members of the traditional ruling class will have nothing to fear . . . The Alliance deserves their support, for is it not a call to their conscience and patriotism and at the same time their very means of self-defense?" The former Venezuelan president, Romulo Betancourt, who was a favourite of the U.S. State Department, has stated in defence of the Alliance: "We must help the poor in order to save the rich."

In other words, the Alliance, even in its original aims, was a neo-colonialist device for forestalling revolutionary change. Its intentions, in fact, were counter-revolutionary.

Because the Alliance for Progress was not predicated on fundamental change, but had the limited aim of patching up the system so as to safeguard American economic and political interests, its six years of operation have resulted in a worsening of the crisis in Latin America. A speech by Robert Kennedy to the United States Senate on May 9, 1966, intended to win support from the hard-hearted senators for conceptions akin to those of the Alliance for Progress, was in itself a confession of the failure of the Alliance. He described Latin America in these critical terms:

"The dependence on only one export product, the relative lack of industry, the absence of a strong internal market and the predominance of governmental monopolies . . . The end-result of this form of development is poverty, degradation, misery whose statistics have become a litany . . . The annual per capita income is under 100 dollars for Latin America . . . The Latin Americans are illiterate. Epidemics and malnutrition prevail in almost all the countries; half of the population of Latin America do not reach the age of 40. To travel in Latin America, seeing the terrible reality of human misery, is to perceive these statistics with annihilating force. In Recife there are people who live in miserable huts near the water, into which they pour their garbage and excrement. The crabs which feed on this filth constitute the base of their nourishing diet. In the nearby fields there are workers who cut cane on the plantations six days a week from sun-up to sun-down to earn U.S. $1.50 per working week . . . And everywhere, around every more or less large city, there are slums, an incredible agglomeration of tin and cardboard, and one-room clay huts through whose door apparently dozens of children come out . . . Those people will not accept these conditions of existence for the next generation. . . . We would not accept them nor will they. There will be changes. A revolution is on the march. A revolution that will be peaceful if we are sufficiently intelligent, moderate if we take the necessary care, successful if we are fortunate, but a revolution that will come whether we want it or not. We can influence its character, but we cannot modify its inevitability."

This is not only an indictment of U.S. control in Latin America, and of six years' working of the Alliance for Progress. It is equally a plea for an adjustment to modern neo-colonialist methods to replace the older forms of domination and exploitation, a plea for reform and the nourishment of local capitalism to avoid the bigger disaster (for the United States) of genuine revolution and a turn towards socialism. Robert Kennedy's warnings on Latin America are an echo of the earlier warnings of Macmillan and De Gaulle on Africa, and of Chester Bowles on Asia; and like them, he pleads for a recognition of the historical forces which are at work and which necessitate the elaboration of new tactics for imperialism, tactics which are intended to "influence the character" of the revolution.

The last few years, however, have shown that the policy of allowing mild concessions and the introduction of moderate reforms is impossible as long as the aim is the defence of American monopoly interests in Latin America. For this reason, those who, in this recent period, have sought the road of reforms, such as Goulart in Brazil, Paz Estenssoro in Bolivia, and Juan Bosch in the Dominican Republic, have been removed by U.S. sponsored military coups, in the latter case by the direct intervention of U.S. troops.

The economic results of the Alliance for Progress, too, show that none of Latin America's basic problems has been solved. In fact, the economic crisis has deepened, while U.S. monopolies continue to make enormous profits.

In the plans of the Alliance for Progress, it was intended that economic development should increase at the rate of 2·5 per cent per capita per year. Though this target was claimed to have been achieved in 1965, James Reston has termed the official figures "somewhat misleading".* First, the overall increase in the first five years of the plan shows an average annual increase per capita of only 1·4 per cent. Secondly, the 1965 figures do not take into account the inflation which has overtaken a number of Latin American countries, and thus the figures, based on inflated prices, hide the real position. Thirdly, Reston stressed, even discounting the effects of inflation, only half of the Latin American countries achieved the planned growth rate, and most of them "actually had a lower growth

* *New York Times*, March 18, 1966.

rate in 1965 than in 1964." Agricultural production actually slowed down over the five years; "the housing deficit is expected to increase"; and educational progress is "not keeping pace with the mounting school population."

The significance of this virtual stagnation has to be seen against the serious decline that characterised the period prior to 1961 when the Alliance for Progress was launched. Latin America's agricultural production only reached its pre-war level in 1956–57. Coal production in Chile dropped from 169,000 metric tons per month in 1954 to 81,000 in 1960. In the same period, coal production in Peru dropped by about fifty per cent—from 21,300 metric tons per month to 14,500. Argentine meat fell from 145,000 metric tons per month in 1956 to 87,000 in 1960. Brick production in Venezuela, gas in Panama, cement in Chile, lead products in Mexico, all showed declines in 1960 and 1961.*

Figures show that the anticipated flow of capital to Latin America through the Alliance has not taken place. Over the first five years only some three quarters of the planned amount has been allocated by the U.S. Congress; and the amount of private capital has not been up to the planned figure either. Furthermore, it has been more than matched by the outflow back to the United States in the form of repatriation of profits from earlier U.S. investments. The pre-Alliance pattern shows that between 1950 and 1960 direct foreign investments in Latin America totalled 6,179 million dollars, while profits transferred abroad totalled 11,083 million, resulting in a net loss to Latin America of 4,904 million dollars. Since the years 1950–1955 cover only profits transferred to the United States, and omit remissions to Europe, it can be safely assumed that the total loss must have been well over 5,000 million dollars.†
The latest figures provided by the U.N. Economic Commission for Latin America (March 29, 1967) show that in 1966 alone

* Gerassi, John: op. cit., p. 379.
† Aguilar, Alonso: "Latin America and the Alliance for Progress"; text of a lecture delivered to the School of Economics of the National University of Mexico, March 10, 1963, New York, 1963.

Latin America paid out 2,140 million dollars in profit and interest on foreign investments.

But it is not a question only of the amounts made available. All the available evidence shows that the sums allocated are mainly spent to aid U.S. interests—to repay debts to the United States, to buy American consumer goods, and to patch up deficits in the balance of payments. (All this, of course, is apart from the amounts taken by the local puppet rulers for their own personal use). Hardly anything is spent on basic economic development. Between 1961 and 1965, only four per cent of the sums allocated went into industrial development, and even that went to U.S. firms already operating in Latin America.*

The question of debt repayment has become a particularly serious problem for Latin America. The general trend is for direct private investments to decline in relation to state loans and credits, and private credits. From 1951 to 1955, Latin American countries received an average of $325 million a year in investments, and $281 million from loans and credits; during 1961–1964 the figures were $293 million and $1,841 million respectively.† The bulk of the loans are actually credits. As John Gerassi has explained, "The money never leaves the United States, while as the loan is paid back, new money enters the United States."‡

The use of the credits is also channelled into serving U.S. interests. As much as 86 per cent of the money is spent for the purchase of U.S. products and services.¶

Latin America's total foreign debts are estimated at 10,000 to 15,000 million dollars. Annual profits remitted overseas in recent years are estimated at 1,000 million dollars; payment for interest on loans and credits, at 400 million; and payments of basic debts, 1,500 million. Thus total annual payments reach 3,000 million dollars—which is more than twice what is

* *Excelsior*, March 15, 1966.
† Sheremetyev, I: "Latin America's Thorny Path to Industrial Development": *International Affairs* (Moscow), December 1966, p. 25.
‡ Gerassi, John: op. cit., p. 270.
¶ *The Vision Letter*, November 12, 1963: Special Supplement.

allocated under the Alliance for Progress, even fifty per cent more than what was planned. The sum paid out each year by Latin America to overseas interests amounts to almost one third of the total value of Latin American exports.

In exchange for such "aid" under the Alliance for Progress, Latin American countries have to agree to "stabilisation" measures. What does "stabilisation" mean?

> "It means more or less frozen wages. It means more or less frozen prices. It means tight credit, a cutback in government spending, a slowdown on expansion. It means, therefore, a halt or near halt in government-subsidised projects and industrialisation. It means, finally, an economy propitious for investors with money—that is, foreign investors. Stability is a distinct advantage to United States corporations investing in the country and for United States buyers of the country's commodity exports. That is why the International Monetary Fund conditions its standby credit to stability or austerity measures."*

The crippling of the economy of Latin American countries in this way puts them increasingly in debt to the United States, and so their dependence grows. Between 1960 and 1965, debts increased fourfold. Debt repayments to the United States in 1965 alone were 2,100 million dollars.

With considerable justice, John Gerassi has commented that the Alliance is between the United States and U.S. businesses in Latin America rather than between the United States and Latin America.

Latin America loses enormously, too, through the non-equivalent exchange of its products with those of the United States and other capitalist powers. Trade with the U.S. alone results in losses of up to 1,500 million a year. The Alliance for Progress had made no difference to the haemorrhage caused in

---

* Gerassi, John: op. cit., p. 273. Dr. Gerassi's reference to 'frozen prices' is not entirely correct, since in many cases 'stabilisation' led, in fact, to serious inflation.

this way. Enrique Caballero Escovar, a Colombian senator, lawyer and big businessman, told John Gerassi:

"The Alliance ends up as just words unless coffee prices are returned to a fair level. We have lost, in the first year of the Alliance, almost twice as much as we have gained from the Alliance . . . When coffee was sold at $1 a kilo we had $53,000,000 a month for our essential imports. Now, we have more coffee to sell, but the price is 41c, and we have only $33,000,000 a month for more imports at higher prices. Pay us good prices for our coffee or—God help us all—the masses will become one great Marxist revolutionary army that will sweep us all into the sea."*

The other aspects of the Alliance have equally failed. Agrarian reform, based on the conception of a gradual transformation of feudal-type latifundias into capitalist-type farms, with a rich peasantry buying their land or making purchases from state lands, leaves the majority of the poor and landless peasants still poor, and still landless. Democracy, far from burgeoning, is under constant attack. The basic semi-feudal structure remains. Dictators flourish. Military rule is commonplace; and the Alliance itself becomes increasingly militarised, with an ever-growing percentage of the appropriations under the Alliance going for military aid.

The people of Latin America, on the basis of six years' working of the Alliance for Progress, can see that the only ones to have made "progress" have been the big U.S. companies and banks, and the puppet dictators who have salted away millions for themselves. Gerassi has estimated that 1,500 million dollars of public funds are stolen from Latin American treasuries *each year*.

Such large-scale corruption and embezzlement, tolerated under the Alliance for Progress, has always accompanied U.S. domination of Latin America. When the dictator Duvalier seized power in Haiti he received 30 million dollars from the United States. In 1961 he was given another 13½ million—

* Gerassi, John: op. cit., p. 295.

equal to nearly half of Haiti's budget for that year. Perez Jimenez, the U.S. backed tyrant of Venezuela until 1958, is estimated to have accumulated 400 million dollars in foreign banks.* His predecessors, Eleazor Lopez Contreras (1935–41) and Isaias Medina Angarita (1941–45) made off with about 13 million dollars each.† Batista is said to have escaped from Cuba in 1959 with 200 million dollars banked overseas. General Trujillo, dictator of the Dominican Republic, "over the years perfected his systematic graft until his annual income was estimated in the neighbourhood of 30 million dollars."‡

The Alliance has made no difference to this tradition.

Meanwhile, in "rich" Venezuela there are 800,000 unemployed, and 300,000 children for whom there are no school places; in Caracas, the capital, 500,000 people live in miserable hovels.

No wonder that Professor Aguilar has called the Alliance for Progress "an instrument in defense of the ruling classes, an expression of Monroeism and an outpost of anti-Communism, an answer to popular discontent, a barricade against any desire for emancipation, an alternative and a check to the Cuban Revolution, and a new Holy Alliance directed against the revolutionary struggle of our people."¶

The very failure of the Alliance for Progress has led the United States to make a new attempt to press ahead with its military plans for counter-revolution in Latin-America. These plans have been maturing over several years, and take two main forms: moves to establish counter-guerrilla forces, and the creation of a continental military force for Latin America controlled by the United States.

The former, commonly known as the U.S. counter-insurgency programme, goes officially by the name of "Special Warfare", for which a section of the Defence Department has been established. By June 1963, according to a speech by

* Andreski, Stanislav: *Parasitism and Subversion*, London, 1966, p. 66.
† Lieuwen, Edwin: *Arms and Politics in Latin America*, New York, 1960, pp. 147–50.   ‡ ibid.
¶ Aguilar, Alonso: op. cit., p. 30.

Robert Kennedy, 57,000 U.S. government officials were being trained in counter-insurgency courses. The main Special Warfare Centre is at Fort Bragg, North Carolina. Here, in addition to training U.S. personnel, courses are organised for selected trainees from the Latin American countries and other foreign states. Five special schools for Latin Americans alone are also maintained in the Panama Canal Zone, under the direct control of the United States Caribbean Command Headquarters. In addition, there is an Inter-American Defense College for Latin American army officers.*

Already, in 1965, the U.S. invasion of the Dominican Republic showed that, alongside the verbal chatter of reforms by means of the Alliance for Progress, the U.S. was prepared to use direct military force wherever the reforms threatened to be radical enough to challenge the existing structure of feudalism and imperialist exploitation. It was at that time that the U.S. President pronounced his doctrine that "the American nation cannot, must not, and will not permit the establishment of another Communist government in the Western Hemisphere" (May 2nd, 1965). Considering that the issue at stake in the Dominican Republic was not communism but independence and democracy, the Johnson Doctrine was clearly directed against any fundamental change in Latin America. At the same time, the direct intervention by U.S. troops in the Dominican Republic led to such an outcry that the Pentagon was driven to intensify its efforts to create an Inter-American Force for use in similar circumstances in the future. The name, Inter-American Force, was, in fact, given subsequently to the U.S. marines sent to the Dominican Republic. To make it a little more plausible, four Latin American countries were persuaded to send small contingents to do duty alongside the preponderantly U.S. troops.

Outwardly, the Inter-American Force is intended to appear as a mainly Latin-American military formation, but in reality

* See Pomeroy, William: *Guerilla and Counter-Guerrilla Warfare*, New York, 1964.

it will be run by the United States. Under the cover of the Inter-American Force the U.S. will be able to continue its role of intervention and counter-revolution. Major-General Max S. Johnson (retired), former planning officer for the Joint Chiefs of Staff, has explained the role of the United States in such a military grouping in an article in *U.S. News and World Report*:

> "Any Inter-American Command set up to prevent the spread of communism in this Hemisphere would almost certainly have to be commanded by a U.S. officer of high rank, with perhaps 98 per cent. of the military means, as well, furnished by the United States."

Between the U.S. intention and achievement, however, there is a considerable gap. The effort to set up such an Inter-American Force has met with a great deal of resistance from the Latin American people, which has found partial expression in the opposition to this idea from most Latin American governments. As a result, the projected military organisation has not yet been established.

In contrast to the various "aid" schemes of the imperialist powers stands the genuine assistance arising from the new economic relations being established between the developing countries and the socialist states. These economic relations rest on an entirely different basis to that between the developing countries and the West. There are no private monopoly firms in the socialist countries which can invest in the Third World, seize possession of land and mineral wealth, establish their own enterprises overseas, and so rob the people of Africa, Asia and Latin America of millions of pounds every year.

Socialist economic agreements are based on complete equality between the two parties. There are no strings attached to such agreements, as has been stressed by Nasser, Sékou Touré and Nkrumah. Socialist credits are provided at $2\frac{1}{2}$ per cent interest, in place of the 6 or 7 per cent usually asked for by the west.* The credits are provided direct to governments, and not to private industry; and the consequence is that the state sector of the economy of the recipient country is strengthened, planning is made easier, and resources can be directed where they are most needed. In addition, socialist credits or loans are repayable over a long term, either in the currency of the recipient country or in its traditional exports; it is not customary for a socialist country to demand repayment in dollars or other western currencies. All blue-prints and patents are provided free. Technicians for new enterprises are usually trained in the course of construction so that by the time the new factory starts operations new technicians in the country concerned can take over control. Socialist loans go, in particular, to help industrial development. Whole plants are exported to developing countries, hydro-electric dams constructed, iron and steel complexes established—but when the machinery is installed and operations begin not a single penny profit is taken out because not a single penny of socialist money is invested; the whole enterprise belongs to the recipient country itself. Such economic relations assist economic growth and independence and so assist the developing countries to offset the attacks of neo-colonialism.

No less than 1,938 different projects have been built, or are in the process of construction, in Africa, Asia and Latin America, with the aid of the socialist countries. By January

* The heavy indebtedness of the developing countries, combined with the contrast of the low-interest credits made by the socialist countries, has compelled the Western powers to modify their interest rates and loan agreements to some extent. Some outright grants are now given, and in some cases interest-free loans; interest is often at 5 to 5½ per cent, as against the previous 6 or 7; and sometimes there is a period of grace before payments of interest commence. Funds provided via the International Monetary Fund are usually at a lower rate of interest, too. At the same time, economic intervention accompanies these loans, the IMF in particular demanding stringent measures to "stabilise" the economy as a condition for receiving a loan. These measures are normally based on "austerity" projects, which result in attacks on living standards and a curtailment of local industrial developments. The economic problems of the developing countries thus remain acute.

1965, the socialist countries had granted credits to Third World countries totalling 5,000 million roubles (i.e. £2,000 million at the official rate of exchange).*

A breakdown of Soviet aid to developing countries gives some indication of its scope and character.† Of some 600 projects for which the Soviet Union was providing assistance at the beginning of 1966 in Africa and Asia, 71 per cent were in industry and geological prospecting. The enterprises included 20 metallurgical plants, 43 machine-building plants, nearly 30 power stations, 16 chemical plants and oil refineries, and 60 enterprises in light and food industries. In the field of higher education and technical training, the Soviet Union is helping to build some 90 colleges and institutes, some of which, as in Guinea, Afghanistan, Burma, and Ethiopia, cater for 1,000 students each. No less than 30,000 Soviet specialists have been sent to assist developing countries; 100,000 skilled workers and foremen have been trained in the developing countries by Soviet technicians; and a further 20,000 people have received industrial and technical training in various Soviet enterprises.

Two examples are sufficient to show how socialist aid assists the developing countries to resist pressure from the West. When the United Arab Republic requested aid from the West to build the Aswan Dam it was refused unless the U.A.R. changed its internal and external policies. When the U.A.R. nationalised the Suez Canal Company to finance economic development, the Western powers launched their attack on Suez. When the attack was defeated it was the Soviet Union which made an agreement to help build the Aswan Dam, granting for this purpose a credit of over £35 million. Guinea, too, has for long been anxious to construct a hydro-electric station on the Konkouré, but Western "capitalist groups . . . held off" writes Prof. Dumont, since they were "not reassured by the political evolution of Guinea."‡ The Soviet Union, however, has

* Kallai, Gyula: *Problems of the World Movement and the International Political Scene*. Based on a lecture in Budapest, 1966. Published Prague, 1967.
† Degiar, D.: *Vneshnyaya Torgovlya*, No. 5, 1966.
‡ Dumont, René: op. cit., p. 107.

agreed to advance credits to Guinea of £30 million to build the power station.

From the foregoing brief examination of the workings of neo-colonialism it can be seen that the all-embracing definitions provided by the All-African People's Conference and the First Tri-Continental Conference are fully borne out. Basically, the various forms of neo-colonialism are intended to fulfil two main aims; to serve the interests—economic, military, political—of external powers; and to create internal conditions in the developing countries which assist the retention of political power in the hands of those social strata which are prepared to co-operate with imperialism and which are best suited to carry through this collaboration. This internal aim is essential to the successful operation of the new tactics of imperialism.

4

The Future of Neo-Colonialism

Imperialism is in retreat. The world is no more its monopoly. But this is only a general truth for the whole epoch in which we live. It does not mean that the imperialists can no longer launch attacks, that they no longer dominate countries, whole regions, or almost entire continents. Not that they no longer have the capacity to cause heavy damage to new young states, or even enjoy important successes, temporary though they may be. As long as imperialism exists the democratic rights of the people, their national independence, their social and economic advance, and world peace itself, are in danger.

The very emergence of neo-colonialism is an expression of the continued capacity of imperialism to intervene in the affairs of other states.

The path of advance for the countries of the Third World is a difficult, tortuous and complex one. Their economies have been distorted by decades of domination by powerful industrial states. Their peoples are largely illiterate. They are beset by widespread disease and undernourishment, by appalling housing, a lack of piped water to villages, a shortage of indigenous technicians.

The overwhelming majority of the people in the Third World are poor peasants, many of them absolutely without land. The working class is relatively small, though growing; industry and urbanisation as yet embrace a minority of the population. Problems of national minorities or tribalism constantly threaten to erupt into open strife. Political parties based on scientific socialism are sometimes absent, or lack experience. Parties which helped their people win independence are an amalgam of social forces which have different conceptions concerning the future development of their countries after independent status had been gained.

It would be strange, indeed, if in such circumstances mistakes were not made, wrong paths taken, inappropriate measures proposed, or incapable people placed in positions of responsibility. Independence, too, has given new opportunities to thousands of individuals overnight to become shopkeepers, small businessmen, administrative officers of the new state, people with new appetites and new possibilities of satisfying them.

It is in such circumstances that neo-colonialism functions and indeed flourishes. Potential allies are sought out, won over by flattery and finance, encouraged to pursue policies which safeguard the bases of imperialist exploitation. Where necessary, strife is stirred up so that the favoured general or police chief or political charlatan can assume control "to end corruption" or "restore law and order". As coup follows coup the people realise that corruption continues, that the restored law is that of privilege and the order that of private profit.

Where the people have established governments which refuse to act as passive supporters of imperialism acute danger is always present. The two decades since the end of the second world war are strewn with the wreckage of parties, guerrilla forces, national movements, and governments which incurred the enmity of imperialism. After 1945, imperialism won temporary success in south Vietnam, south Korea, Malaya, the Philippines. In the last ten years, pressure from the right has given new opportunities for neo-colonialism in Ceylon and India. An appalling massacre, in which anything up to a million communists and other patriots have been slaughtered, has brought back the foreign monopolies and western advisers to Indonesia. Lumumba was murdered in Congo (Kinshasa), Ben Bella removed in Algeria, and Nkrumah overthrown in Ghana. Communists have been under constant attack by reactionary governments in the Sudan; and Oginga Odinga and other progressive leaders of the Kenya People's Union are being persecuted by a Kenya government from which has been excluded practically everyone who played a leading part in the struggle for independence. In Iraq, the people's victory of 1958 was succeeded by a ghastly coup in which thousands lost their lives. Across the Atlantic, the People's Progressive Party Government has been ousted from office in Guyana; Goulart's government deposed by a military coup in Brazil; and a democratic victory in the Dominican Republic prevented by open U.S. intervention. In many other states, in Asia, Africa and Latin America, supporters of neo-colonialism have been in power from the very moment of independence.

It would therefore be foolish to underestimate the strength of neo-colonialism. Imperialism is by no means finished. The majority of new states of Africa and Asia and practically the whole of Latin America are still subject to its influence, in some cases almost completely so. Neo-colonialism is not simply imperialism in retreat, but imperialism finding a new basis on which to continue its activities in the Third World. The fact that it has found this new form, despite its being an expression of a weakened position, shows that it is not yet exhausted, not yet defeated.

Nevertheless, if neo-colonialism gives a new lease of life to imperialism, and provides a new opportunity for imperialist activities to continue, it is, from an historical standpoint, only a temporary phenomenon. Just as colonialism created its own gravediggers—the national movement of the overwhelming majority of the people—so neo-colonialism creates it own new grave-diggers, with their sharpened edge turned against capitalism itself. Hundreds of millions of people, the majority of mankind, commented Lenin,* "are now coming forward as independent, active and revolutionary factors". For this reason, he said, "it is perfectly clear that in the impending decisive battles in the world revolution, the movement of the majority of the population of the globe, initially directed towards national liberation, will turn against capitalism and

* Lenin, V. I.: Report to Third Congress of the Communist International, July 5, 1921, *Collected Works*, Vol. 32, pp. 481-2.

imperialism and will, perhaps, play a much more revolutionary part than we expect."

The gravediggers which colonialism created were the working class, the dispossessed and poor peasantry, the new intelligentsia, and the national bourgeoisie. By trying to prop up and preserve feudalism and other pre-capitalist forms of society, colonialism undermined its own prestige and positions as well as those of its local allies. By introducing a money market linked to imperialism it made possible the beginnings of an indigenous capitalism. By creating an educated cadre for its state administration, local government, commercial houses and schools, it produced a force from which would emerge a patriotic group of "Young Turks" eager to win independence and propel their countries into the twentieth century. By compelling a section of peasants to become workers it began a process of severing millions from the old closed village economy, with all its superstititions and restricted horizons, transforming peasants into an urbanised stratum of wage earners who formed trade unions, organised strikes, acquired a class and political consciousness, and began to think in terms of a radical change of society.

At first, it was possible for colonialism to continue on the basis of such a class structure, clinging for as long as was possible to the forces of the old order—the Ashanti chiefs in Ghana, the Moslem emirs in Nigeria, the Rajahs in India, the Sheikhs in the Middle East, the Sultans in Indonesia. But in a world which is turning from capitalism to socialism, and which is witnessing an unprecedented growth of the movement for national liberation and the collapse of the old forms of colonial rule, pre-capitalist forces can no longer be the permanently preferred choice of imperialism. The Moroccan Al Glaoui, the feudal prop of French colonialism, has made way for King Hassan, the capitalist prop of neo-colonialism. The Rajahs of India have been replaced by the Indian National Congress, by the monopoly capitalist firms of Tata and Birla. The Shah of Iran finds it necessary to introduce land reforms and other measures which weaken the basis of feudalism.

Of course, the turn from feudalism to capitalism is nowhere simple or absolute. Continued British support for the feudal sheikhs of South Arabia, and for the monarchies of Saudi Arabia and Jordan shows only too well that imperialist reliance on such allies has in no sense been ended completely. In any case, a certain merging is taking place between the feudal landlords and the new capitalist traders and entrepreneurs.

Just as colonialism creates its own gravediggers which prevent it being a stable, long-term system, so neo-colonialism does the same. By nourishing the forces of capitalism while preventing their full fruition it creates a weak capitalist class which is increasingly revealed as being incapable of solving the problems of the people. Such a weak class is a prey to inner conflict and rivalry which results in instability and the constant danger of military coups. The further growth of the working class which accompanies this partial spread of capitalism in the new states, coupled with the failure of neo-colonialism and the indigenous bourgeoisie to provide the majority of the people with a better life, results in the whole neo-colonialist structure being called into question.

Modern colonialism was only a temporary phase. In less than a century it was destroyed by a changing world and by a growth of new class forces burgeoning within the womb of the colonial system itself. Surplus value can no longer be pumped out sufficiently from the Third World on the old colonial and feudal basis. New rulers and local capitalist forces, alongside rival imperialisms which can now penetrate into the former colony previously maintained as a closed monopoly by the colonial power, all want their share of the surplus being wrung from the workers and peasants—and this at a time when the workers and peasants themselves are demanding and expecting a better life than before, and when millions of new mouths are crying to be fed. Pre-capitalist forms of economy, feudal institutions, old societies are inadequate to meet these new demands.

Neo-colonialism, too, will be but a temporary phase; and

again, not only because the world moves but because neo-colonialism itself gives rise to new internal contradictions and conflicts, and to new forces which will resolve them. The very propping up of capitalist forces which co-operate with imperialism and make neo-colonialism possible, leads to the undermining of the political prestige and influence of such sections which become more and more exposed as neo-colonialism's ally, whether willing or unwilling. At the same time, the growth of capitalism results in new sharp points of conflict between the interests of this class and of imperialism, which leads to the instability of the alliance and of the regimes themselves, challenged, as they are, by a growing working class. On the land, the growing differentiation among the peasantry, the emergence of a richer farmer class employing wage labour, and the further breakdown of the village economy, creates a vast army of landless peasants, of semi-proletarians whose poverty and misery can never be ended under this twisted system which has neither destroyed feudalism nor created mature capitalism.

Colonialism never rested on a local basis of "normal" feudalism, but on a mutilated and distorted system, with a few capitalist adornments; and neo-colonialism in no sense rests on complete capitalism but on a restricted, stunted and controlled form which weakens the very capitalist rulers on whom it depends for maintaining its influence.

Neo-colonialism may last for a period of years in a number of territories. It can do considerable damage to the prospects of fundamental social and economic change in the Third World. It can grant imperialism a breathing space, provide a partial stabilisation and a new reinforcement and enrichment to the world of capitalism.

Nevertheless, it is constantly rent by its own weaknesses and contradictions which will increasingly tear it asunder. The past fifteen years have already seen the demise of neo-colonialist governments in the United Arab Republic, Cuba, Zanzibar, Congo (Brazzaville), Burma, and Syria, overthrown by revolutionary forces which, in varying degrees, have commenced to destroy the very roots of imperialism and to break up the foundations of those feudal and capitalist forces on which neo-colonialism depends.

The transition from neo-colonialism to liberation will not necessarily always require the armed revolutionary overthrow of a puppet government. Sometimes it will take place as a result of the slow maturing of events, and the unfolding of a whole series of measures—social, economic and political—which lead, stage by stage, to the transformation of society. In some cases, the leaderships which have come to power as a consequence of the winning of national independence—and especially in states where both feudalism and capitalism were exceptionally weak—will find it possible to embark along a road which severely restricts neo-colonialist activity, as is happening in Guinea, Mali and Tanzania. In other cases, as in Ghana and Indonesia, advances along such a road were made, only for neo-colonialism to strike back and regain some of its lost positions. Similar imperialist offensives may yet be tried, even with success, in other territories.

For the peoples and their parties in the countries of the Third World it is not enough to denounce neo-colonialism; nor to proclaim the aim of socialism. Basic to defeating neo-colonialism and completing liberation is the creation of an independent economy. This is a task which requires a whole series of measures to take the resources and enterprises into national hands; to create a state sector of the economy, establish basic industrialisation, state control of trade, and ownership of banking and insurance; to carry through a fundamental land reform which ends landlordism, gives land to the landless, and introduces diversification and the modernisation of agriculture. A planned economy, based on proportioned development, can allocate sums each year for the people's welfare even while accumulating the necessary funds for industrial development. People will not tolerate for long the ostentation and luxury-living of the new élite.

Where governments already led by revolutionary democrats are in power the necessary political measures can be taken to realise these economic tasks. Essential to these policies is the democratic mobilisation of the people, the encouragement of working class participation in planning and management, the right of workers to establish their own trade unions without state or party interference, and of the peasants to set up their co-operatives for distribution and production.

The price of liberty is eternal vigilance. The experience of neo-colonialism shows that for the peoples of the Third World exceptional vigilance is required. This demands the establishment of new state organs after the withdrawal of colonial rule —an army, intelligence and police force based on tried and tested opponents of colonialism and imperialism and not on well-groomed, brain-washed and Western-oriented trainees from Sandhurst, St. Cyr and Fort Bragg.

The political and administrative sides of the state also have to be staffed; and for these posts, too, genuine patriots and democrats are needed. Asian, African or Latin American civil servants who are more English than the English, or more French than the French, or more American than the Americans, are unlikely to prove the most consistent and effective opponents of neo-colonialism.

In most countries, the defeat of neo-colonialism will require, as an essential first step, the defeat of its internal ally, and the removal of governments which are collaborating with imperialism; in a number of cases, this will involve armed conflict.

To conduct the many-sided struggle which the above tasks involve, the people of the Third World find that they require a strong revolutionary party, closely linked to the workers and peasants, winning the support of the progressive intelligentsia and other patriots, and based on a scientific understanding of the modern world and the laws of its motion.

Neo-colonialism is a world-wide phenomenon; it cannot be defeated by the people of each country acting in isolation. It requires the united effort of all anti-imperialist forces—the socialist countries, the national liberation movements, and the working class and democratic movement in the imperialist countries.

In the years that lie ahead the people of the Third World

face sharp and bitter struggles. The emergence of neo-colonialism is a proof that imperialism will fight desperately to safeguard its investments and its possibilities of exploitation. But with each day the forces opposed to it become stronger.

We live in an epoch of transition to socialism which will embrace all countries, whether large or small, and no matter how undeveloped at present may be their economy and social life. Already one third of mankind has cast off the shackles of imperialism and capitalism and is blazing a trail to the future. The world socialist system, which encompasses more than one thousand million people, constitutes, together with the national liberation and democratic movements of the rest of the world, the determining force of our time. Imperialism, however desperately it strives to avert its defeat and however much damage it inflicts, can no longer decide the fate of mankind. The peoples are on the march; and their growing insistence that colonialism in all its forms be ended will prevail.

Bibliography

Afrifa, A. A.: *The Ghana Coup*, London, 1966

Ainslie, Rosalynde: *The Press in Africa*, London, 1966

Andreski, Stanislav: *Parasitism and Subversion*, London, 1966

Barraclough, G.: *An Introduction to Contemporary History*, London, 1964

Bowles, Chester: *The Conscience of a Liberal*, New York, 1962

Castro, Josué de: *Geography of Hunger*, London, 1952

Cohen, Sir Andrew: *British Policy in Changing Africa*, London, 1959

Cox, Idris: *Socialist Ideas in Africa*, London, 1966

Dankwortt, Dieter: *On the Psychology of German Development Aid*, Bonn, 1962

Dumont, René: *False Start in Africa*, London, 1966

Dutt, R. Palme: *The Crisis of Britain and the British Empire*, London, 1953

Fanon, Frantz: *The Damned*, Paris, 1963

Gerassi, John: *The Great Fear in Latin America*, New York, 1965

Isaacs, Harold R.: *No Peace for Asia*, 1947

Jagan, Cheddi: *The West on Trial*, London, 1966

Kahin, G. M.: *Nationalism and Revolution in Indonesia*, Ithaca, 1952

Kintner, Wm. R.: *National Security. Political, Military and Economic Strategies in the Decade Ahead*, New York, 1963

Krause, Walter: *Economic Development—Underdeveloped World and the American Interest*, San Francisco, 1961

BIBLIOGRAPHY

Lee, Clark: *One Last Look Around*, New York, 1947

Lenin, V. I.: *Draft Theses on the National and Colonial Question*, June 1920
Imperialism—the Highest Stage of Capitalism, 1916

Lieuwen, Edwin: *Arms and Politics in Latin America*, New York, 1960

Lodge, George Cabot: *Spearheads of Democracy—Labour in the Developing Countires*, New York, 1962

Mansur, Fatma: *Process of Independence*, London, 1962

Mao Tse-tung: *On the People's Democratic Dictatorship*, Selected Works Vol. 4, Peking edition, 1961

McCune, George, M.: *Korea Today*, Cambridge, Mass, 1950

Morris, George: *C.I.A. and American Labour*, New York, 1967

Nkrumah, Kwame: *Africa Must Unite*, London, 1963
Neo-Colonialism, The Last Stage of Imperialism, London, 1965

Pomeroy, William: *Guerrilla and Counter Guerrilla Warfare*, New York, 1964

Reno, Philip: *The Ordeal of British Guiana*, New York, 1964

Roy, Ajit: *Economics and Politics of U.S. Foreign Aid*, Calcutta, 1966

Scheer, Robert and Zeitlin, Maurice: *Cuba, An American Tragedy*, London, 1964

Scheer, Robert: *How the United States Got Involved in Vietnam*, California, 1965

Stalin, J. V.: *The October Revolution and the National Question*

Tinker, Hugh: *South Asia*, London, 1966

Wise, David and Ross, Thomas B.: *The Invisible Government*, New York, 1964

Woddis, J.: *Africa—The Lion Awakes*, London, 1961
Africa—The Roots of Revolt, London, 1960

Index